HEALTHIER STEPS

125 Gluten-Free Vegan Recipes

Copyright 2014 Michelle Blackwood

Grubb
Blackwood
PUBLISHING

— For my Family —
This book is dedicated to my four taste testers, my loving husband, and my children Devannah and Daevyd.

Contents

FOREWARD

Funny how like-minded individuals attract! Upon meeting Michelle, we realized there was something a little different and very special about her. As two foodies might, we almost immediately started talking nutrition and she told us about her book. She not only practices what she preaches, but does it with an irrepressible joy that can only come from one who has done it and is passionate about the results.

This is by far one of the best cookbooks we have read. It is perfect for anyone who is interested in making a serious change in their diet and may be daunted by the idea of preparing gluten-free alternatives. She includes tons of great information about ingredients, which helps to unlock the mystery, explaining what many of the more obscure ingredients are, their purpose and where to find them. Having read and studied nutrition extensively, many authors seem to assume that everyone knows what these things are and where to find them! Quite frankly as health coaches, we think finding these things and truly understanding why you use them is half the battle for many people. Michelle's research is top-notch and with her medical background to back her up, she brings an additional flare to the table.

Having travelled and lived for many years abroad, she accesses an outstanding variety of international flavors that will stimulate any palate that is adventurous enough to join her on her 'healthier-steps' journey. The anecdotal stories are particularly engaging as she shares how many of the recipes came to be as inspired through her travel. In truth, once we started the book, we couldn't put it down!

We hope and pray as you read and use this excellent resource that you will be blessed with the abundant health that is sure to come from feeding your body with the riches of the whole foods that are so-often neglected. Bon Appetit!

— *Drs. Robert and Laura Sparks, DC*

INTRODUCTION

Thank you for being a part of my journey in achieving better health through healthy eating. This journey started 15 years ago, when my husband and I decided to study better ways of achieving a healthier lifestyle. Our research led us in making a decision to completely remove meat from our diet. We did so gradually, by first deciding to remove red meat, then chicken, fish and finally dairy products. After a few months of our new diet, we felt great and noticed an increase in energy. Many of the symptoms I had, including sinusitis problems and panic attacks disappeared. Now my new vegan life has made me thankful that my husband and I started this journey together.

My passion for cooking and entertaining has led me to spend a lot of time in the kitchen experimenting on new dishes. Seeing that I was born and raised in Jamaica, I'm greatly influenced by a Jamaican style of cooking that results in flavorful dishes. I have also been influenced by my travels to Europe and other Caribbean islands. The positive responses over my cooking that I continued to receive from my guests, friends and family were overwhelming. It was this encouragement that has kept me continuing my research and experiments with plant-based meal ideas.

Five years after my journey began, our family moved to a missionary college and for the next 10 years I had a great opportunity to cook vegan and entertain students from countries all over the world. I also started sharing my new found way of eating by doing cooking classes and health lectures.

This has had the most impact on my cooking repertoire of ingredients, dishes and style. I also remembered the years I was away from home while in college, living abroad and longing for home-cooked meals. I remembered the wonderful people that invited me to their homes for a nice home-cooked meal. So I took the opportunity to give back. I not only gave the students meals from my own country of Jamaica, but I made sure I prepared dishes from their native countries as well. It took me hours of research and shopping trips to international supermarkets, but it was very rewarding. I enjoyed the challenge and the gratitude of the students.

My decision to start my vegan blog, HealthierSteps.com, came three years ago after first recovering from carpel tunnel syndrome, a near death experience in 2009, and a year later, a bout with IBS (Irritable Bowel Syndrome). I had had my share of ill health and wanted to share about how I used natural foods for my healing and recovery, by eating a vegan diet, and using herbal remedies.

When I had my first episode with IBS, I did not realize that gluten was the culprit. During my first episode, my doctor had me go on a juice diet for three weeks. My symptoms—stomach cramps, bloating, constipation, and diarrhea—went away. I gradually progressed to a regular vegan diet, and noticed that the symptoms returned, but not as severe as the first episode, after eating foods containing gluten. It was way later that I made the full connection and decided to totally remove gluten from my diet so my intestines could heal. My blog then naturally progressed to include gluten-free recipes.

I transformed my pantry into one that is gluten free. I then started experimenting more and more with recipes and fell totally in love with the results. Now, I can "have my cake and eat it, too." As I shared the recipes with my friends and family, I noticed that they too enjoyed the recipes. I decided to make gluten-free granola and cookies which I packaged and sold both at my local farmer's market and online.

Eating a gluten-free and vegan diet actually enlarged my culinary experiences and took me to another level. I now incorporate more healthy whole grains such as quinoa, sorghum, buckwheat grouts, teff, and millet in our diet with their additional nutritional benefits.

I am now ready to open up my kitchen and its pantry to you and share over 125 of my delicious gluten-free and vegan recipes. I know you'll love them all.

Gluten is a group of proteins, gliadin and glutenin found in grains (gliadin is the protein that gives the most problems). They are the thick, glue-like proteins that make foods stick together when baked. These proteins are found in wheat, barley and rye. Gluten is a very difficult protein to digest and may cause insensitivity and/or a severe reaction in some people when consumed. This undigested gluten results in the destruction of the villi (hair-like projections) that line the intestines. This gluten sensitivity varies from a mild gluten sensitivity/intolerance to more severe cases causing celiac disease. That means that everyone with celiac disease is gluten sensitive/intolerant. But one can be sensitive/intolerant without having celiac disease. Celiac disease is an autoimmune disease where the body reacts to the gluten protein as a foreign invader and attacks itself. Symptoms include diarrhea, bloating, constipation, blood in the stool, psoriasis, anemia and acne. The body's response to gluten varies from person to person, so every symptom may not manifest itself in an individual. This poor absorption of nutrients can result in malnutrition. Normally, those who experience these symptoms find that their symptoms go away after removing gluten from their diet.

ABOUT THE RECIPES/SUBSTITUTE INGREDIENTS

All the recipes in the book are gluten-free and vegan. They are all made from plant-based ingredients.

Most of my recipes contain ingredients you already have in your kitchen. Although I love to include exotic dishes with unfamiliar ingredients, I do offer substitution ideas and or places where these ingredients can be purchased. So whether you are a beginner vegan or you are seasoned and are just looking for recipes to challenge your creativity, this cookbook is for you.

BRAGG'S LIQUID AMINOS — A soy sauce alternative that eliminates the process of fermentation. It can be substituted for soy sauce, tamari or coconut aminos in the recipes throughout the cookbook.

COCONUT PALM SUGAR — A natural sugar that is made from the sap of the coconut palm tree. This sap is heated until most of the liquid has evaporated.

EGG SUBSTITUTES — I have had success with using both flax seeds and chia seeds as egg substitutes. I prefer to use the golden flax seeds or the white chia seeds for aesthetic purposes. Do not use the pre-ground varieties; buy the whole seeds and process as needed using a spice grinder or a blender. You can use either chia seeds or flax seeds or half and half in the recipes. Also, consume a lot of water when eating products with these seeds.

HERBS — I prefer to use fresh herbs rather than dried herbs, which is why I grow most of my herbs. When not in season though, I will to resort to dried herbs. Substitute 1 part dried herb for 1 part fresh.

NUTRITIONAL YEAST FLAKES — This is de-activated yeast that has been grown on enriched pure cane and beet molasses. It imparts a delicious, cheesy flavor to prepared dishes, and also contains vitamin B12.

OATS — I included oats as the ingredient does not naturally contain gluten, but a protein similar to gluten called avenin. However, oats can get cross-contaminated by other gluten containing grains. Five percent of people suffering with celiac disease are not able to tolerate oats, due to avenin being a similar protein to gluten. For the remaining people who react to gluten, it's best to purchase certified gluten-free oats.

POTATO FLOUR — is made by grinding the whole potato. It has a distinct cream color and it does looks more grainy than potato starch. It is best used in savory, gluten-free baked goods because of its taste. It can also used as a thickener for soups, gravies and stews.

POTATO STARCH — is an extracted starch that comes from potatoes; it is a very fine white starch that has a neutral taste and is excellent used as a thickener for gravies, soups, and stews. It is also great in gluten-free baking, producing a light, tender and moist crumb in cakes.

PURE MAPLE SYRUP — is three times sweeter than regular sugar and also contains less calories. To substitute maple syrup for sugar in regular cooking, replace 1 cup of sugar with ¾ cup of maple syrup. You will also use the same amount in your baking as well as reducing the amount of liquid in your recipe. Also, you will need to reduce recipes by 3 tablespoons of liquid to every cup of maple syrup use. Using equal amounts when substituting honey or agave with maple syrup. Therefore, 1 cup of maple syrup would call for 1 cup of honey instead. I only use pure maple syrup and coconut palm sugar in all the recipes in this book.

NUTS — Wherever nuts are used in the cookbook, they are raw unless noted otherwise. The cashew nut is the preferred nut to use in this cookbook, its mild taste, smooth and creamy texture easily enhance the dishes. If you have a high speed blender almond nuts may be substituted. Without the use of the high speed blender, the resulting dish may be grainy and less desirous. Feel free to experiment with whatever nuts or seeds that are easier to find in your location. Depending on your recipe, almonds, pine nuts, hazelnuts and macadamia nuts can be substituted in desserts. Pumpkin seeds, sunflower seeds, walnut, pecan, almond, Macadamia, pine nuts and hemp can be substituted in your savory dishes. For almond meal/flour throughout the book, I made my own by processing with a high speed blender.

CORN — The issue of GMO (genetically modified organism) is a big topic here in the USA, but 61 countries worldwide have either banned GMO foods or implement laws for the labelling of GMO foods. I included a few recipes containing organic corn such as corn bread, for those who aren't affected by GMO corn. Feel free to leave out corn in recipes that do contain corn or its by-products, substitute cornstarch with equal amounts of potato starch, tapioca starch, or arrowroot starch in your recipes. Please note that if you are allergic or have sensitivity to corn, the following products may contain hidden corn: xanthan gum, baking powder, powdered sugar, brown sugar (caramel color). Certified organic corn and corn products (cornflour, cornstarch, cornmeal) can be purchased in health food stores or online.

SALT — Although I have listed the amount of salt I used for most of the recipes, you should season to your taste. I used pink Himalayan salt for all my recipes, but you are able to use sea salt, which is better than table salt because it doesn't contain additives such as dextrose and silicon dioxide found in table salt.

TAPIOCA STARCH/FLOUR — the white starchy extract of the yucca or cassava root. It has a slightly sweet flavor and it is used in gluten-free baking as a substitute for wheat. It adds texture or chewiness to baked goods. It is also used as a thickener instead of cornstarch.

HOW TO COOK BEANS/LEGUMES

Beans, legumes and peas are an important source of protein, carbohydrate, and fiber in a plant-based diet. They are relatively inexpensive, have a long shelf life, there are thousands of varieties, and they very versatile in creating delicious recipes.

To sort beans, spread beans on a baking sheet in a single layer and remove ones that are broken, discolored or shriveled. Using a colander, rinse with cold water. Place beans in a large bowl and cover with water at least 3 inches above beans. Soak overnight. The following day, drain beans and rinse with cold water. Add enough water to cover beans, about an inch above. Bring to a boil, then reduce to a simmer and cook until beans are tender. Pierce a bean with fork to test if tender. Cooking times vary depending on the type of beans.

If you don't have time to soak beans overnight, you can try the quick soak method. Place the sorted and washed beans in a large saucepan, cover with water and bring to a boil for about three minutes. Cover saucepan, remove from heat and allow to soak for one hour.

Avoid adding salt, tomato juice or vinegar during the cooking process. The addition of these ingredients prevents the beans from absorbing water. These ingredients should be added after the beans are completely cooked. Soaking the beans before cooking helps to remove the indigestible complex sugars that result in gas and bloating as well as tannins, trypsin inhibitors, and phytic acid.

To store dried beans, legumes and peas, store in an airtight container and keep in a cool, dry, dark place. If done properly, beans will last for up to one year.

Refrigerate cooked beans for up to 3-5 days, or store for six months in the freezer in an airtight freezer container.

HOW TO COOK GLUTEN-FREE GRAINS

Measure grain, sort and remove debris. Transfer to a fine mesh strainer and rinse under cold running water. Place grain in a large pot with tight fitting lid, add the desired amount of water and bring to a boil. Reduce heat, cover and simmer for the desired amount of time needed for the grain to cook until tender. Fluff with a fork once all the liquid is absorbed. Replace the cover, remove from the heat and allow to sit for 10 minutes. A pinch of salt may be added to cook the grains. Note that you can also soak grains for one to eight hours to increase digestibility.

Gluten-Free Grains	Nutritional Content	Cooking Gluten-Free Grains
Amaranth	High in protein (complete protein), calcium, magnesium, phosphorus, potassium and vitamin C.	1 cup grain to 3 cups water. Cooks for 30 minutes. Sprinkle cooked amaranth on salads, add to soups, pancakes, porridge or in baked goods.
Buckwheat	Not a true grain, nor is it related to wheat as its name implies. It is actually a fruit seed belonging to the rhubarb and sorrel family. Buckwheat is a rich source of protein, fiber. The high levels of rutin in the leaves are extracted for medicine to treat high blood pressure.	1 cup buckwheat groats to 2 cups of water. Cooks for 20 minutes. Delicious as breakfast cereal, pancake or served as a stuffing.
Cornmeal	Cornmeal is produced by drying corn and then grinding it into a meal. It provides a rich source of fiber, potassium, niacin, magnesium, phosphorus and iron.	1 cup cornmeal to 3 cups water. Cook for 20 minutes. Served as a cooked breakfast cereal, as a savory polenta or in baked goods.
Millet	Millet is not just for birds, but is a nutritious grain. It is a good source of magnesium, phosphorus, manganese and copper.	1 cup millet cooks with 2 cups water for 30 minutes. Delicious as a breakfast cereal, in breads, or sprinkled in soups or salads.
Oats, Rolled	Rich in beta glucan, a soluble fiber which lowers cholesterol. Oats also contain phosphorus, selenium, manganese, zinc, vitamin E and carotenoids.	1 cup rolled oats with 3 cups water. Cook for 20 minutes. Served as a hot or cold cereal, in vegetable burgers, breads, cookies and muffins.

Gluten-Free Grains	Nutritional Content	Cooking Gluten-Free Grains
Quinoa	Not a real grain, but the seed of an herb. A complete protein, high in fibers, iron, vitamin B-complex, magnesium, potassium, and calcium.	1 cup quinoa cooks with 2 cups water for 20 minutes. Rinse before cooking. Delicious served as a salad bowl, with soups, beans or as a filling.
Brown Rice	A good source of fiber, protein, iron, folate, zinc, selenium and vitamin B-complex.	1 cup rice to 2 cups water for 40 to 60 minutes. Delicious served alone or in paella, stuffed peppers, soups, casseroles.
Sorghum	A good source of fiber, magnesium, calcium, niacin and iron.	1 cup of sorghum grain to 3 cups of water. Cook for 50-60 minutes. Excellent in baked goods, breads or wraps due to its slightly sweet flavor.
Teff	Excellent source of fiber, protein, iron, phosphorus, copper, calcium and vitamin C. It doesn't contain phytic acid like other grains.	1 cup teff grain to 3 cups water for 15-20 minutes. Delicious in pilaf, stews, teff flour is delicious in breads, pancakes, and muffins.
Wild Rice	Contains a good source of protein, fiber, magnesium, phosphorus, zinc, and folate.	1 cup wild rice to 3 ½ cups water for 60 minutes. Served as a stuffing, with other grains, or pilaf.

HOW TO SAUTE WITHOUT OIL

Heat 1 to 2 tablespoons of broth or water in a stainless steel skillet over medium heat. Once the broth begins to bubble, add onions and sauté, stirring frequently. After the onions have cooked for about 5 minutes, you can then add other ingredients, such as garlic or fresh ginger. Once they have had a chance to cook together for just another minute or two, add other vegetables. This method enables you to have flavorful sautéed vegetables without heating oil.

You can reduce the amount of oil in your recipes. For instance, if the recipe calls for 1 tablespoon, you can reduce the amount to 1 teaspoon and add 1/4 cup of vegetable broth. You can also use 1/4 cup of vegetable broth alone to substitute for all the oil in the recipe.

MY FAVORITE KITCHEN TOOLS

Mason Jar — I love to use mason jars for my smoothies, drinking my lemon water in the morning and throughout the day, as a sprouting jar for seeds, nuts and grains, to store homemade nut butters, and cheese sauces, homemade spice mixes, and homemade barbecue sauce.

Food Processor — For processing burgers, pates and making pie crusts.

Chef's Knife — Invest in a sharp knife; it is actually safer than a dull knife.

Baking Sheets — Great for baking cookies, fries, burgers, patties and roasting vegetables.

Blender — This is a must have in a gluten-free, vegan kitchen. A high-speed blender such as Blendtec is a beneficial investment. It is capable of making nut-based sauces creamy and delicious, which would otherwise be gritty and unpalatable with a standard blender.

Muffin Pans/Cake Pans — Excellent for your muffins and cupcakes.

Large Saucepan/Skillet — I love to use stainless steel pans or ceramic non-stick pans.

Juice Extractors — Great for extracting enzyme and nutrient-rich fruit and vegetable juices. I like the Champion juicer and Breville juicer.

Citrus Reamer — Used for juicing oranges, lemons and limes.

Stainless Steel Pots, Pans — They are definitely better for your health than aluminum.

Parchment Paper — Used to line aluminum baking sheets, loaf pans, and cake pans. Excellent to prevent food from sticking when lightly oiled.

Cooling Rack — Perfect for cooling baked goods. They allow air to circulate freely, reaching all sides of your cooking, breads or muffins.

Ice Cream Scoop — Stock all sizes for filling muffin pans, forming cookies, for making burgers and veggie meatballs.

Can Opener — for opening coconut milk and canned beans.

Measuring Spoons and Cups — for getting exact measurements.

Fine Mesh Strainer — for washing quinoa and other fine grains.

MY GLUTEN-FREE VEGAN PANTRY

GRAINS/PASTAS

Brown jasmine rice	Long grain brown rice
Old fashioned rolled oats	Quinoa
Brown rice pasta	Quinoa pasta

GLUTEN-FREE FLOURS/STARCHES

Non-GMO corn flour/cornmeal	Brown rice flour	Chickpea flour
Sorghum flour	Potato flour	
Millet flour	Quinoa flour	
Potato starch	Tapioca starch	

BEANS/LEGUMES

Lentils (black, green and red)	Black beans
Red kidney beans	Black-eyed peas
White Cannellini beans	Butter beans
Lima beans	Chickpeas
Split peas	Edamame

NUTS

Pine nuts	Raw Cashews
Walnuts	Almonds

SEEDS

Chia seeds	Flax seeds
Sesame seeds	

DRIED HERBS AND SPICES

Thyme	Oregano	Coriander	Allspice	Dill
Basil	Marjoram	Cardamom	Tarragon	Fennel
Paprika	Turmeric	Cumin	Cayenne Pepper	

OILS

Extra virgin olive oil
Coconut oil
Sesame oil

SWEETENERS

Maple syrup	Dates
Coconut palm sugar	Molasses

EXTRAS

Bragg's liquid aminos/soy sauce/coconut aminos	Nutritional yeast flakes	
Canned coconut milk	Canned beans	Vanilla extract
Baking powder	Canned tomatoes	Almond extract

BREAKFAST

Breakfast is the most important meal of the day. It gets your body's metabolism going after its fast (sleep). It sets the tone for the rest of the day. People who eat breakfast are more likely to lose weight. Research also shows that people who eat breakfast score better on tests, are more alert and have better attitudes.

ALMOND CRANBERRY GRANOLA

YIELD: 8 SERVINGS

Making your own granola is very easy, plus you have the power to unleash your creativity by deciding what goes into your recipe. Feel free to add your favorite dried fruits, nuts or seeds to this recipe.

INGREDIENTS:

4 cups (384g) gluten-free rolled oats
½ cup (30g) unsweetened coconut flakes
¼ cup (26g) flax seeds, ground
¾ cup (180ml) maple syrup
¼ cup (60ml) coconut oil, melted
1 cup (125g) almond slivers
1 cup (160g) fruit juice sweetened cranberries
1 teaspoon almond extract
1 teaspoon vanilla extract
1 teaspoon sea salt

DIRECTIONS:

Preheat oven to 250°F and line a baking sheet with greased parchment paper. In a large bowl, combine rolled oats, coconut flakes, and flax seed. In a saucepan on medium, heat maple syrup, coconut oil and sea salt, stirring constantly for 2 minutes. Remove from heat and add almond and vanilla extract. Mix wet ingredients into oat mixture and coat evenly. Spread thinly onto baking sheet. Press down granola with the palm of your hands and bake for 1½ hour, turning every 30 minutes. Cool, then add almond slivers and cranberries. Store granola in an airtight container.

Chef's Tip: I like to make a double batch and bake at 170°F for 8 hours.

There is nothing like the smell of banana muffins baking in the morning. Wake your family up to these moist and delicious muffins. Use fully ripened bananas and coconut palm sugar to add extra sweetness. This is way better than traditional recipes that call for about twice the amount of refined sugar.

INGREDIENTS:

2 tablespoons ground flax seeds or chia seeds
¼ cup (60ml) almond milk
1 cup (140g) brown rice flour
2/3 cup (128g) potato starch
1/3 cup (35g) almond flour
½ cup (96g) coconut palm sugar
2 teaspoons baking powder
½ teaspoon sea salt
¾ cup (180ml) almond milk
2 tablespoons coconut oil, melted
2 teaspoons vanilla extract
2 bananas mashed
½ cup (50g) walnuts, chopped

DIRECTIONS:

Preheat oven 350°F/175°C. Line muffin pan with 12 paper liners, lightly greased, and set aside for 4 minutes. In a small bowl, mix ground flax seeds with ¼ cup almond milk and set aside. In a large bowl, mix brown rice flour, potato starch, almond flour, coconut palm sugar, and sea salt. In a medium bowl, mix together, ¾ cup almond milk, coconut oil and vanilla.

Combine liquid ingredients along with flax seed mixture with dry ingredients until fully mixed. Fold in mashed bananas and walnuts until just blended. Fill muffin tins to about 2/3 full, and bake for 25 minutes or until toothpick inserted in center comes out clean. Remove from pan and serve immediately or transfer to a cooling rack for 5 minutes.

These yummy biscuits are crispy on the outside and buttery with the use of virgin coconut oil. Delicious served with hot brown rice gravy.

INGREDIENTS:

¼ cup (26g) flax seed meal
¼ cup (60ml) water
½ cup (70g) brown rice flour
½ cup (56g) almond flour
¼ cup (30g) tapioca starch
¼ cup (48g) potato starch
2 teaspoons baking powder
¼ teaspoon sea salt
¼ cup (60ml) almond milk
1 tablespoon coconut palm sugar
¼ cup (60ml) coconut oil

DIRECTIONS:

Preheat oven 425°F/218°C. Stir together flax seed meal and ¼ cup water and allow to sit for 5 minutes to gel. Combine brown rice flour, almond flour, tapioca starch, potato starch, baking powder and salt in a large bowl, mixing well. In a medium bowl, mix almond milk, coconut palm sugar and coconut oil. Add wet ingredients to dry ingredients, stir in flax seed gel and mix until fully combined. Place dough into a ½ cup measuring cup or ice cream scoop and transfer onto a greased or parchment lined baked sheet. Bake for 12-15 minutes or until golden brown. Allow the shortcakes to cool, slice them horizontally with a serrated knife.

BLUEBERRY BUCKWHEAT PANCAKES

These are delicious and easy to make, wonderful served with blueberry sauce, applesauce or maple syrup. If you don't have millet flour, try substituting corn flour, sorghum flour or quinoa flour.

INGREDIENTS:

½ cup (60g) buckwheat flour
½ cup (60g) millet flour
1 tablespoon ground flax seeds
1 ½ teaspoons baking powder
¼ teaspoon sea salt
½ cup (120ml) non-dairy milk (almond, soy, coconut, or rice)
2 tablespoons maple syrup
1 teaspoon vanilla
1 banana, mashed
½ cup (55g) blueberries
Coconut oil for greasing skillet
Blueberry sauce (recipe follows)

DIRECTIONS:

Combine flax seeds and hot water in a bowl and set aside for 3-5 minutes to thicken. In a large bowl, mix buckwheat flour, millet flour, baking powder and sea salt together. In a separate bowl, combine milk, flax mixture, maple syrup and vanilla. Add wet ingredients into dry ingredients, mixing well. Fold in banana and blueberries. Heat a greased skillet or non-stick griddle over medium heat. Using a ¼ cup measuring cup, place pancake batter onto skillet or dry griddle and flatten with back of a large spoon. Cook for 3 minutes, then flip and cook for 2 minutes more. Serve with blueberry sauce.

Chef's Tip: For a lighter pancake, make the batter thinner by adding extra non-dairy milk, stirring well.

INGREDIENTS:

2 cups (220g) blueberries
¼ cup (60ml) maple syrup
1 tablespoon tapioca starch and 2 tablespoons water mixed well.

DIRECTIONS:

Heat water, blueberries, and maple syrup in a saucepan on medium heat, stirring and bruising some of the blueberries. Stir together tapioca starch and water in a small bowl. Stir tapioca starch mixture into blueberries and continue to stir until sauce thickens. Remove from heat and serve.

Chef's Tip: You may substitute arrowroot powder or non-GMO cornstarch, or just cook the sauce on a low flame, stirring until it thickens.

BLUEBERRY MUFFINS

YIELD: 12 MUFFINS

Use fresh, frozen or dried blueberries. I love to pick blueberries from the farm. I get to eat some fresh, add some to smoothies and pies, and freeze the rest. I added applesauce in this recipe to add extra flavor and moisture to the muffin. Instead of cinnamon, I used a combination of coriander and cardamom to give a different spin from the norm. Maple syrup adds a delicate and sweet flavor to the muffins.

INGREDIENTS:

2 tablespoons flax seed meal
¼ cup (60ml) almond milk
1cup (140g) brown rice flour
½ cup (56g) almond flour
½ cup (96g) potato starch
2 teaspoons baking powder
1 teaspoon coriander
Pinch ground cardamom
½ teaspoon sea salt
½ cup (120ml) applesauce
¼ cup (60ml) almond milk
½ cup (120ml) maple syrup
¼ cup (60ml) coconut oil, melted
1 teaspoon vanilla
¾ cup (82g) blueberries

DIRECTIONS:

Preheat oven 350°F/175°F. Line and grease nine muffin cavities with muffin liners, and fill the remaining three with water. In a small bowl, mix flax seed meal and almond milk. Set aside. In a large bowl, combine rice flour, almond flour, potato starch, baking powder, coriander, cardamom, and sea salt. In a medium sized bowl, mix applesauce, almond milk, maple syrup, coconut oil and vanilla. Add wet ingredients into dry ingredients and mix well. Fold in blueberries. Using a ¼ cup measuring cup, fill muffin tins and bake for 25-30 minutes until tops are golden brown or until toothpick inserted into the center comes out clean.

Carob powder comes from the pulverized seed pod of the carob tree, a Mediterranean evergreen shrub. It is mildly sweet and caffeine free, unlike chocolate, which contains theobromine, a substance that is poisonous to some mammals. Carob powder is high in insoluble fibers, which speeds the passage of waste through the colon. It also helps to prevent constipation. It is high in antioxidants, which prevents free radical damage to the cells. It is also high in calcium and iron. Carob powder and chips can be purchased at health food stores or online.

INGREDIENTS:

2 tablespoons ground flax seeds
¼ cup (60ml) almond milk
1 cup (140g) brown rice flour
½ cup (56g) almond meal
½ cup (48g) carob powder
2 teaspoons baking powder
½ teaspoon sea salt
½ cup (120ml) maple syrup
¼ cup plus 2 tablespoons (80g) almond milk
¼ cup (60ml) coconut oil, melted
2 teaspoons vanilla extract
½ cup (80g) carob chips (optional)

DIRECTIONS:

Preheat oven 350°F/175°F. Line and grease nine muffin cavities with muffin paper, fill the remaining three with water. In a small bowl, mix ground flax seeds and almond milk and set aside. In a large bowl, stir in brown rice flour, almond meal, carob powder, baking powder, sea salt. In a medium bowl, mix maple syrup, almond milk, vanilla extract. Mix wet ingredients with dry ingredients. Fold in carob chips. Using ¼ measuring cup, add batter to muffin pans and bake for 30 minutes. Remove from oven and let pan sit for 10 minutes.

My first encounter with crepes was on my first visit to Paris over 20 years ago. I was in awe and intrigued at the art of crepe making as I stood to watch a Parisian street vendor skillfully make batch after batch of this delicate pancake.

INGREDIENTS:

Sauce
½ cup (62g) raw cashews
¾ cup (180ml) water
2 tablespoons nutritional yeast flakes
2 teaspoons onion, chopped
1 clove garlic
1 teaspoon lemon juice
1 teaspoon arrowroot powder
1 teaspoon sea salt

Steamed Asparagus
1 pound asparagus
1 cup (240ml) water
¼ teaspoon sea salt, optional

Crepes
2/3 cup (75g) buckwheat flour
1/3 cup (rolled oats, ground
2 tablespoons potato flour
A pinch of sea salt
1 cup (240ml) non-dairy milk (almond, rice or soy)

DIRECTIONS:

In a blender, add raw cashews and water, and process until smooth. Add nutritional yeast flakes, onion, garlic, lemon juice, arrowroot and sea salt and continue to blend until smooth. Transfer sauce to a medium saucepan, heat on medium high. While stirring, cook until bubbly.

Preparing asparagus: Wash asparagus spears, cut about an inch off the bottom of spears and discard. Bring water to boil in a large pot, and place asparagus in a steaming basket. Place basket over water, cover asparagus and cook for about 5-7 minutes or until tender.

Preparing crepes: In a large bowl, combine buckwheat flour, oat flour, potato flour, and sea salt. Stir in non-dairy milk using a wire whisk. Heat skillet on medium high and lightly brush with oil. Add about ¼ cup of batter to the pan. With a large spoon, swirl the batter in the pan to coat the bottom of the skillet evenly. Cook for about one minute and bubbles should appear all over the surface. Using a spatula and fingers, flip the crepe over and cook the other side until dry. Transfer onto a platter, and cook remaining batter.

To Assemble: Arrange 6-8 asparagus spears in the middle of each crepe, pour some of the sauce on top of the asparagus. Fold crepes over to enclose asparagus and place seam side down. Top with extra sauce and serve immediately.

Chef's Tip: Note that the recipe calls for potato flour and not potato starch. They are two different products.

Buckwheat flour is gluten-free and it is from a whole seed; it is not related to wheat.

This dish provides a healthy and delicious alternative to soy. Chickpeas, like tofu, are very versatile and can be used in dishes that you would normally use tofu, such as soups, salads, and stir-fry. It absorbs the flavors of what it is cooked in, similar to tofu. Chickpeas contain a good source of protein, fiber, iron, potassium, vitamin B-6 and magnesium.

INGREDIENTS:

2 tablespoons olive oil, plus extra for sautéing
1 pound (454g) chickpea tofu, cut into cubes (recipe below)
½ cup (80g) onion, finely minced
2 cloves garlic, minced
¼ cup (39g) red bell pepper, diced
¼ cup (39g) orange bell pepper, diced
½ cup (15g) loosely packed spinach, chopped
1 tablespoon nutritional yeast flakes
Sea salt to taste

DIRECTIONS:

Heat oil in large skillet on medium heat. Add chickpea tofu and sauté until golden brown, for about 5 minutes. Turn once and cook the other side until golden brown and crisp. Remove to a dish and set aside. Add onion, garlic and bell peppers to the skillet. Cook until onion is soft, about 4 minutes. Stir in spinach, tofu, yeast flakes and salt, cook for 2 minutes then serve.

INGREDIENTS:

1 cup (120g) chickpea flour/garbanzo flour
1 teaspoon sea salt
Pinch turmeric
3 cups (720g) water, divided
1 teaspoon coconut oil

DIRECTIONS:

Lightly grease 8 (20cm) x 8 (20cm) inch square baking dish with oil, set aside. Bring 1 ½ cups water to boil in a medium pot. Meanwhile, combine chickpea flour, sea salt, and turmeric with the remaining 1 ½ cups water, and whisk until no lumps remain. Add chickpea flour mixture to boiling water, whisking constantly. Reduce heat to medium low, whisking continuously for about 5 minutes until mixture thickens with a shiny gloss. Pour immediately into prepared dish. Allow to cool, then refrigerate until set, at least 2 hours.

Recipe adapted from: The Burmese Kitchen: Recipes from the Golden Land by Copeland Marks and Aung

Chef's Tip: Chickpea flour may be purchased from an Indian grocery or at a health food store. It is also called besan flour.

DATE WALNUT SCONES

INGREDIENTS:

2 tablespoons ground flax seeds
¼ cup (60ml) almond milk
1 cup (96g) rolled oats (gluten-free)
½ cup (70g) brown rice flour
½ cup (56g) almond meal
¼ cup (30g) tapioca starch
¼ cup (48g) potato starch
¼ cup (48g) coconut palm sugar extra for sprinkling
1 tablespoon baking powder
½ teaspoon sea salt
¼ cup (60ml) cold coconut oil, cut in pieces
½ cup (120ml) almond milk
¼ cup (60ml) maple syrup
1 tablespoon orange zest
2 teaspoons vanilla extract
½ cup (50g) walnuts, chopped
½ cup (75g) dates, chopped

DIRECTIONS:

Preheat oven 375°F/190°F. Lightly grease a parchment lined, 9-inch skillet and set aside. In a small bowl, mix together ground flax seeds and almond milk, and set aside. In a large bowl, whisk together brown rice flour, almond meal, tapioca starch, potato starch, coconut palm sugar, baking powder, and sea salt. Cut in coconut oil using a pastry blender, two knives or fingers, until mixture is crumbly. In another small bowl, mix together almond milk, orange zest, and vanilla extract and stir into the flour mixture until combined. Fold in walnuts and dates.

Transfer dough into skillet and sprinkle the top with coconut nut palm sugar. Bake in oven for 25-30 minutes or until golden brown and firm to touch. Remove skillet from oven and allow scones to cool for around 10 minutes.

When I first arrived in the USA from England, I lived in New Jersey. I soon realized that bagels were more popular there than scones. At the time, I missed scones and clotted cream, but as time passed, I had to settle for bagels and cream cheese. Later on, I stopped eating dairy and then started shopping at Whole Foods Market, where I fell in love with their vegan date walnut scones, which reminded me so much of the scones I had in England. As time went by I could no longer eat products with gluten, so I had to find another alternative for scones. In this recipe, I believe I nailed the recipe or at least come very close to the ones I had at Whole Foods. Well, at least they satisfy my longing without the terrible upset stomach.

Fried or boiled dumplings are a Jamaican staple. They are easy to make and are usually served as a side with ackee and saltfish and callaloo. Not only are mine gluten free and dairy free, they are also cooked with less oil than the traditional method.

INGREDIENTS:

2 tablespoons golden flax seed meal
¼ cup (60ml) almond milk
½ cup (70g) brown rice flour
½ cup (50g) corn flour
2 tablespoons potato starch
2 tablespoons tapioca starch
1 teaspoon baking powder
¼ teaspoon sea salt
¼ cup (60ml) almond milk
2 tablespoons coconut oil

DIRECTIONS:

In a small bowl, mix flax seed and almond milk and set aside for 5 minutes. In a large bowl, combine brown rice flour, corn flour, potato starch, tapioca, baking powder, and sea salt. Add the remaining almond milk and flax seed mixture and stir. Knead dough into a large ball. The ball should be smooth; if it's too sticky, add more corn flour. If the dough is too dry, add a little extra almond milk.

Set a large non-stick skillet on medium heat and add coconut oil. Shape dough into small balls (about 8), then flatten balls slightly.

Place dumplings in heated skillet, and cook until golden brown. Carefully turn dumplings over, using a fork, and cook other side until golden brown. To cook remaining dumplings, you may need to add extra oil.

Chef's Tip: To use the minimum oil recommended, I use a ceramic non-stick pan, then I cook dumplings on one side, turning on the other side then cover skillet and finish cooking on low heat. To test if they are done, tap dumplings and they should have a hollow sound.

Cooked sweet potato balances the glycemic level of diabetics. It is high in vitamin A, which boosts the immune system, protects and repairs the skin from sun damage, giving the skin a healthy glow. The fiber content is twice that of other potatoes. A diet high in fiber enhances bowel function, lowers cholesterol and helps to control blood sugar. It is an excellent nutrient for improving vision and repairing macular degeneration.

INGREDIENTS:

1 tablespoon olive oil or ¼ cup water
1 medium onion, chopped
2 garlic cloves, finely chopped
2 medium sweet potatoes, peeled and cut into bite-sized pieces
4 cups (268g) kale, stems removed and chopped
1/3 cup (75ml) water
1/3 cup (180ml) coconut milk
Pinch of dried thyme
¾ teaspoon sea salt or to taste

DIRECTIONS:

Heat oil or water in a large saucepan on medium heat. Add onion and sauté until soft, about 4 minutes. Stir in garlic and cook for 30 seconds. Add potatoes and kale, and stir to coat. Add water, coconut milk, and thyme. Cover and cook for 20 minutes, stirring occasionally until potatoes are tender.

These flavorful sausage patties are great for breakfast, lunch or dinner. The fiber in oatmeal is beneficial for lowering cholesterol and blood pressure, slowing digestion time, reducing risk of colon cancer, preventing constipation and increasing the feeling of fullness.

INGREDIENTS:

2 cups (480ml) water
3 tablespoons liquid aminos or soy sauce
2 tablespoons nutritional yeast flakes
1 teaspoon onion powder
½ teaspoon sea salt
½ teaspoon rubbed sage
½ teaspoon garlic powder
½ teaspoon paprika
¼ teaspoon celery seeds
¼ teaspoon fennel seeds
¼ teaspoon cumin
¼ teaspoon Italian seasoning
¼ cup (25g) walnut, ground
2 teaspoons maple syrup
¼ cup (30g) oat flour
2 cups (160g) gluten-free quick oats

DIRECTIONS:

Preheat oven 400°F/200°C, grease baking sheet and set aside. Bring water to boil in a medium saucepan, add soy sauce, nutritional yeast flakes, onion powder, sea salt, sage, garlic powder, paprika, celery seeds, fennel seeds, cumin and Italian seasoning. Stir in walnuts, oat flour and maple syrup. Add quick oats, stirring, and remove from heat. Cover saucepan and let sit for 20 minutes. Form oat mixture into sausage links or patties. Bake on baking sheet for 30 minutes, turning halfway.

25

Nothing like these gooey and delicious orange-infused sweet rolls with cardamom spice, drenched in refreshing orange coconut icing.

INGREDIENTS:

Wet Ingredients
½ cup (120ml) almond milk
2 tablespoons golden flax seed meal
2 tablespoons psyllium seed husk powder
½ cup (120ml) orange juice
¼ cup (60ml) maple syrup
¼ cup (60) coconut oil, melted
1 teaspoon vanilla
1 teaspoon orange zest

Dry Ingredients
1 cup (140g) brown rice flour
1 cup (192g) potato starch
½ cup (56g) almond meal
½ cup (60g) tapioca starch
2 teaspoons baking powder
½ teaspoon sea salt

Filling
¼ cup (60ml) coconut oil
¾ cup (144g) coconut palm sugar
¼ cup (15g) shredded coconut
1 teaspoon coriander
¼ teaspoon cardamom
1 orange zest
Orange Coconut icing
1 (14-ounce/400ml) can full fat coconut milk
¼ cup (60ml) maple syrup
1 orange zest
¼ cup (60ml) orange juice

DIRECTIONS:

Preheat oven 400°F/200°C. Grease pan of choice and set aside. In a medium bowl, combine almond milk, flax seed, psyllium husk\ powder, orange juice, maple syrup, coconut oil, vanilla and orange zest. In a large bowl, combine brown rice flour, potato starch, almond meal, tapioca starch, baking powder and sea salt. Add liquid ingredients to the large bowl, mix well to combine. Dough will be slightly sticky. Roll out dough between two sheets of parchment paper. Remove parchment paper, then mix filling ingredients in a bowl, and spread on top of dough, leaving ½ inch perimeter without filling.

Roll up the long way, pinching the seam closed. Cut one inch rolls with sharp knife. Lay rolls on cut sides up on pan. Bake for 20-25 minutes. Allow to slightly cool, then pour icing over sweet rolls.

To make Icing: Heat coconut milk, maple syrup, orange juice, vanilla and orange zest on medium heat and bring to a boil. Reduce heat and simmer for 30 minutes, stirring occasionally until thickened. Remove from heat and cool slightly.

This hearty breakfast is a great way to start the morning. The high fiber and protein content of quinoa will keep you feeling full longer and help suppress food cravings. You can top with your favorite fruits, and try stirring in a tablespoon of ground flax seed or chia seeds.

INGREDIENTS:

1 cup (184g) quinoa
1 cup (240ml) water
1 cup (240ml) almond milk
¼ teaspoon ginger, finely grated
3 tablespoons maple syrup
½ teaspoon vanilla extract
Pinch of sea salt (optional)
1 pear, chopped
¼ cup (25g) walnuts, chopped

DIRECTIONS:

Rinse quinoa with cold water and drain liquid using a fine mesh strainer. Place quinoa, water, almond milk and ginger in a medium saucepan and bring to a low boil. Cook uncovered for about 20 minutes, stirring constantly. Removed from heat and stir in maple syrup, vanilla, sea salt, chopped pear and walnut.

Tofu is a delicious egg substitute for vegans. I decided to include soy in my cookbook because I believe my cookbook will be used by people outside the United States (at least in my birth country, Jamaica). Here in the USA, most of our soy (about 91%) is genetically modified, and as of the time of writing this book, there is no law for labeling foods containing GMO's. Soy is a major source of protein, and in countries like China and Japan, people consume soy products daily without the adverse issues we face here.

I included Chickpea Scramble Tofu in this book for those desiring an alternative to soy.

INGREDIENTS:

1 pound (454g) extra firm organic tofu, mashed
¼ cup (12g) nutritional yeast flakes
1 ½ teaspoons granulated onion
1 teaspoon sea salt
 ½ teaspoon dried thyme
½ teaspoon cumin
½ teaspoon turmeric
1 tablespoon coconut oil or ¼ (60ml) cup water
½ onion, minced
2 cloves garlic, minced
¼ cup (39g) red bell pepper, diced

DIRECTIONS:

In a bowl, combine mashed tofu, yeast flakes, onion powder, sea salt, thyme, cumin, and turmeric and set aside. On medium high heat, heat oil or water in a large saucepan. Add onion and cook until soft. Stir in garlic and cook for 30 seconds. Add bell pepper and cook for 2 minutes, stirring often. Add seasoned tofu and cook, stirring constantly for about 8 minutes.

SIMPLE BROWN RICE PANCAKE

These pancakes are not to be taken lightly, although they are easy to prepare. They are very light and fluffy. One of the advantages of living in the countryside is that I get to pick wild raspberries which are bursting with flavor.

INGREDIENTS:

1 cup (140g) brown rice flour
½ cup (56g) almond meal
¼ cup (30g) tapioca starch
¼ cup (48g) potato starch
2 tablespoons golden flax seed or white chia seeds
1 ¼ cups (200ml) water or non-dairy milk
2 tablespoons maple syrup
2 teaspoons baking powder
½ teaspoon sea salt
½ teaspoon vanilla
Raspberries for garnishing

DIRECTIONS:

In a large bowl, combine brown rice flour, almond meal, tapioca starch, potato starch, ground flax seeds, baking powder, and sea salt. In a smaller bowl combine milk, maple syrup and vanilla. Thoroughly combine wet ingredients into dry ingredients. Heat oiled skillet on medium high heat, pouring in ¼ cup batter. Cook for approximately 3 minutes, then flip and cook for about 2 more minutes. Repeat until batter is used up.

Chef's Tips: Remember: don't confuse potato starch for potato flour; they are different! Also, I used a ceramic, non-stick skillet.

Dosa is a South Indian fermented pancake that is traditionally served for breakfast with sambar or chutney. It's usually made with a combination of rice and urad dal. In this variation, I chose to use only urad dal and I also did not allow it to ferment.

INGREDIENTS:

1 cup (150g) urad dal soaked
½ cup (120ml) water
½ teaspoon sea salt
1 tablespoon coconut oil

DIRECTIONS:

Wash and soak dal for 4 hours or overnight in water. The following day, drain and rinse dal. Place dal, water and salt in a blender and process until smooth and creamy. Heat a non-stick skillet on medium high heat, lightly oil skillet. Pour ¼ cup batter and spread as thin as possible. Cook on one side for about 2 minutes until brown, then turn dosa onto the other side. Repeat with the remaining batter.

Chef's Tip: For dosa use skinned and split urad dal found in Indian supermarkets, it looks creamy white.

These waffles are quick and easy to make and, best of all, they freeze very well. So go ahead and make an extra batch of these healthy whole grain waffles. They are delicious served with blackberry sauce. I make blackberry sauce from wild blackberries growing near our home. These sweet and juicy organic blackberries are a real treat.

INGREDIENTS:

1 cup (140g) brown rice flour
½ cup (68g) sorghum flour
½ cup (60g) gluten free oat flour
1 tablespoon golden flax seed meal
2 teaspoons baking powder
½ teaspoon sea salt
1 ¼ cups (200ml) non-dairy milk (almond)
¼ cup (60ml) maple syrup
1 teaspoon vanilla
Blackberry sauce
2 cups (220g) blackberries
¼ cup (60ml) maple syrup
¼ cup (60ml) water divided
1 teaspoon tapioca starch
1 teaspoon lemon juice
1 teaspoon vanilla
Pinch of salt (optional)

DIRECTIONS:

Preheat waffle iron. In a large bowl, combine brown rice flour, sorghum flour, oat flour, ground flax seeds, baking powder, and sea salt. In a smaller bowl, mix together milk, maple syrup and vanilla. Whisk wet ingredients into dry ingredients until mixture is smooth. Brush waffle iron with oil, put 1/3 cup batter for each waffle, cover and cooked until golden brown, about 3-5 minutes, depending on the machine. Repeat with remaining batter. Delicious served with blackberry sauce and coconut whipped cream.

Blackberry Sauce: Put berries, maple syrup and 2 tablespoons of water in a medium saucepan and bring to boil. Reduce to a simmer, stirring often, for 4 minutes. In a small bowl, stir the remaining 2 tablespoons water with tapioca starch, lemon juice, vanilla and salt until tapioca starch dissolves. Add to berries and stir until thickened.

Chef's Tip: These waffles may be refrigerated or frozen for later use by placing in airtight freezer bags.

31

BEVERAGES

SMOOTHIES

I love to include smoothies in my meal plan, especially when I'm busy, or when I feel run down and tired. It's a fast way to get lots of nourishment in a meal. It boosts my immune system and is full of antioxidants, which fight diseases.

BANANA ALMOND FLAX SEED SMOOTHIE

INGREDIENTS:

1 frozen banana
1 cup (240ml) almond milk
1 tablespoon ground golden flax seed
1 teaspoon maple syrup

DIRECTIONS:

Place ingredients in a blender and process until smooth. Serve immediately.

It's breakfast time, yet this smoothie tastes like pie with the addition of coconut palm sugar.

INGREDIENTS:

½ cup (125g) pumpkin puree
½ banana
½ cup (120ml) lite coconut milk or almond milk
1 tablespoon coconut palm sugar
¼ teaspoon ginger, freshly grated
¼ teaspoon vanilla
¼ teaspoon coriander
Pinch of cardamom

DIRECTIONS:

Place all the ingredients in blender. Process until smooth and adjust sweetener to taste. Serve immediately.

DANDELION SMOOTHIE

YIELD: 2 SERVINGS

Dandelion is not just a pesky weed growing in your yard. It is actually a superfood and herbal medicine. It increases liver function, bowel function, is a diuretic, slows the growth of tumors, regulates blood sugar and insulin levels, and stimulates the appetite.

INGREDIENTS:

1 cup (240ml) water
1 cup (67g) dandelion leaves
1 banana (frozen)
1 cup (165g) pineapple
1 apple
1 inch ginger
2 tablespoons flax seed
Scant amount of maple syrup, honey or stevia (optional)

DIRECTIONS:

Place all the ingredients above in a high speed blender and process until smooth and creamy.

Caution: Use only leaves picked from a pesticide-free lawn. If you have gallbladder disease, don't use dandelion without medical approval.

I love to add maca in my smoothies. It increases my energy without the side effects of caffeine. Maca root originates from the Andes and has been used to boost immune systems and increase stamina for centuries.

INGREDIENTS:

2 cups (480ml) almond milk
2 cups (60g) spinach
1 cup (165g) pineapple
2 frozen bananas
1 apple
1 tablespoon flax seed
1 tablespoon maca powder

DIRECTIONS:

Place all ingredients in a high speed blender and process until smooth. Serve immediately.

This recipe is for the beginner. It is creamy and sweet, and the taste of the spinach is very mild.

INGREDIENTS:

2 cups (480g) almond milk
2 cups (60g) spinach
1 frozen banana
1 pear
1 apple
1 tablespoon flax seeds (optional)

DIRECTIONS:

Place all the ingredients in a blender and process until smooth.

This smoothie has a delicious tropical flair, with pineapple, coconut, and banana. Enjoy the taste of the tropics with this antioxidant packed smoothie.

INGREDIENTS:

½ cup (82g) pineapple juice
½ cup (120ml) coconut milk
½ cup (55g) blueberries
1 frozen banana

DIRECTIONS:

Place pineapple juice, coconut milk, blueberries and banana and process until smooth.

Serve immediately.

Health Tip: The colorful blue pigments in blueberries, called anthocyanins, are an antioxidant that has been found to slow down vision loss, lower blood pressure, improve memory, strengthen bones, and prevent cancer in clinical studies.

Chef's Tip: Blueberries freeze well without damaging the anthocyanin antioxidants, according to studies; so go ahead and stock up so you can enjoy them all year long.

INGREDIENTS:

1 cup (240ml) almond milk
1cup (165g) mango
Pinch of cardamom
5 ice cubes (optional)

DIRECTIONS:

Peel and chop mango. Place mangoes in a blender, add almond milk, and cardamom.

Blend until smooth.

Chef's Tip: Choose mangoes with a sweet, fruity, fragrant aroma. When ripened, mangoes will be yield gently to pressure when touched, like avocado and peach. Mangoes that are still hard can be placed in a brown paper bag and be left on the counter to ripe, in a few days. Mangoes can be peeled, deseeded, sliced and stored in an airtight container or plastic freezer bag for up to 12 months.

INGREDIENTS:

1cup (240 ml) almond milk
1 peach, pitted and chopped
1 frozen banana, chopped
1 handful of spinach
½ inch ginger

DIRECTIONS:

Blend the almond milk, frozen banana, peach, spinach and ginger until very smooth.

Serve immediately.

Chef's Tip: Smoothies that contain nuts as protein are a great addition to your weight loss plan and may be beneficial as a meal replacement. They are a healthy substitute for empty calorie drinks such as sodas, providing nutrients and fiber to keep you full longer.

During the hot summer months, when watermelon is in abundance, I love to make watermelon ginger beer. This delicious treat is just so easy to create. Try to use very sweet watermelon; then you can eliminate the sugar.

INGREDIENTS:

4 cups (616g) of watermelon chunks
1 inch ginger
1 lime juice
2 tablespoons coconut palm sugar (optional)

DIRECTIONS:

Place watermelon chunks in blender along with ginger, lime juice and sugar and process until smooth. Serve immediately.

JUICES

Juicing fruits and vegetables is another method used for supplementing the body with lots of nutrients. With juices the fibers are removed and only the liquid remains, therefore the body has nothing to break down leading to faster absorption of nutrients. Juicing allows much greater intake of nutrients than eating fruits and vegetables. Some benefits of juicing, weight loss, glowing skin and hair, increased energy, improved digestion and mental clarity.

This juice is pleasant to drink; it is packed with nutrients that will cleanse and build the blood. It contains potassium, calcium, phosphorus, iron, magnesium, folic acid, and vitamins A, B complex, and K.

INGREDIENTS:

1 medium beet, including greens
1 handful of spinach
1 cucumber
1-2 green apples
1 inch ginger root
1 celery stalk

DIRECTIONS:

Wash vegetables and juice using a juice extractor. Drink immediately or store in a tight-fitting glass jar in the refrigerator.

Dandelion, popularly known as a tenacious weed that loves our lawns, is actually a very beneficial herb with numerous healing properties. It is cultivated as an herb in Germany, France, China, and recently the USA. The leaf is approved in Germany to be used to stimulate appetite and to treat an upset stomach. The root is also approved for the treatment of bile flow disturbance, such as in conditions like hepatitis, jaundice, and cirrhosis of the liver, and is a diuretic.

INGREDIENTS:

6 leaves of dandelion
1 cucumber
1 stalk of celery
2 apples
½ inch ginger

DIRECTIONS:

Wash and chop ingredients as needed to fit in the juicer feed. Juice and drink immediately.

Caution: Use only leaves picked from a pesticide-free lawn. If you have gallbladder disease, don't use dandelion without medical approval.

This delicious raw juice is a much healthier version of the store-bought, pasteurized version. This raw version is full of nourishing vitamins, minerals and living enzymes.

INGREDIENTS:

1 beet
½ red bell pepper
6 carrots
4 tomatoes
2 stalks celery
A handful of spinach
¼ cup (40g) onion, diced
1 garlic
Sea salt to taste (opt)
Cayenne pepper (opt)

DIRECTIONS:

Wash and chop ingredients so they fit in the juicer feed. Juice and drink immediately.

INGREDIENTS:

6 carrots
A handful of kale or other green, leafy vegetable
1 lemon

DIRECTIONS:

Wash the above ingredients thoroughly and cut into small pieces that can be fitted into your juicer. Put the leaves in first; the carrots and lemon will help to push the leaves through the juicer. Drink your juice right away for maximum potency or store in a glass jar with an airtight lid to conserve its nutrients for up to 24 hours.

NON-DAIRY MILKS

Non-dairy milk alternatives are especially wonderful for those with lactose intolerance and milk allergies. There are many non-dairy milks on the market nowadays. Many of them are highly processed and they contain ingredients that causes health problems. For example, carrageenan, a common additive extracted from seaweed, is believed to cause inflammation in our bodies. Chronic diseases, such as cancer, diabetes, Parkinson's disease, and Alzheimer's disease, are as a result of inflammation in the body. Making your own milk is a solution for you and your family to minimize the risk of their possible side effects.

This is my favorite non-dairy milk for use in breakfast cereal. I also love to use coconut milk in my savory recipes. You can omit the dates.

INGREDIENTS:

1 cup (225g) almonds
4 cups (960ml) water
6 dates, pitted
1 teaspoon vanilla flavoring
Pinch of sea salt (optional)

DIRECTIONS:

Sort and soak almonds in water for 8 hours or overnight. (I find that when I soak the almonds they are easier to blend and digest better). Rinse almonds, and place in blender with water.

Blend until smooth, then strain the milk through a fine mesh strainer or cheesecloth.

Put the milk back into the blender, along with dates (If dates are not soft, they may be soaked for 10 minutes in warm water), vanilla and sea salt. Blend again until smooth.

Almond milk should be stored in a container with a tight-fitting lid and kept for up to 3 days in refrigerator.

Health Tip: Almond milk is a milk substitute used since the Middle Ages. It is high in the antioxidant vitamin E, which may help to prevent cancer and slow the aging process. It is high in omega-3 fatty acids, which lowers the levels of 'bad' LDL cholesterol and protects your heart. It contains calcium, which helps to strengthen bones. It has a high concentration of vitamins and minerals, compared to soy and rice milk. It is low in fat and calories: one cup of almond milk contains 60 calories, compared to 146 calories in whole milk.

COCONUT MILK

Coconut can be sweetened by adding sweetener of your choice (date, cane sugar, maple syrup, coconut palm sugar or honey), vanilla and pinch of sea salt. Plain coconut milk adds flavor to curries.

INGREDIENTS:

4 cups (960ml) hot water (not boiling)
2 cups (120g) unsweetened coconut flakes

DIRECTIONS:

Heat water and place coconut in blender and blend on high for several minutes, until thick and creamy. Pour the coconut milk through a fine mesh strainer or cheesecloth to strain. Discard the pulp. Drink immediately or keep refrigerated for up to 4 days.

Unlike dairy milk, cashew milk is cholesterol free. Cashews are high in B vitamins, copper, calcium and magnesium. Cashews contain mostly unsaturated fatty acids, which support a healthy heart and can help lower your risk of heart disease and strokes.

INGREDIENTS:

1 cup (125g) raw cashews
3 cups (720ml) water, divided, plus more for soaking
2 tablespoons maple syrup
2 teaspoons vanilla
Pinch sea salt

DIRECTIONS:

Cover raw cashews overnight in water, then drain and rinse. Place cashews in a blender along with one cup of water and process until smooth. Add maple syrup, vanilla, sea salt, and remaining water. Blend until creamy, then strain milk using a fine mesh strainer or cheesecloth. Refrigerate. Will keep in refrigerator for about 5 days.

Chef's Tip: Cashews should smell nutty and sweet. To prevent the oils from going rancid, store raw cashews in a tightly sealed glass jar in the refrigerator for up to six months.

A delicious caffeine-free alternative to the sugar-loaded hot chocolate. It tastes so good on cold wintry nights.

INGREDIENTS:

1 cup (240ml) almond or cashew milk
1 tablespoon maple syrup
1 tablespoon carob powder
1 teaspoon grated ginger
¼ teaspoon alcohol-free vanilla

DIRECTIONS:

In a small saucepan, whisk in the carob powder into the milk until smooth and free of lumps. Heat on medium, but remove from heat before it boils. Stir in ginger, vanilla and maple syrup.

Health Tip: Carob is a legume, also known as St. John's bread and locust bean. It originates from the Mediterranean region. It is a healthier alternative to chocolate, with a sweeter flavor. It does not contain the caffeine and theobromine found in cocoa. Caffeine and theobromine are stimulants that can cause adverse reactions such as heart disease, insomnia, sleep disturbances, bed-wetting, diabetes, depression, obesity, acne, palpitations, agitation, birth defects, and cancer. Carob is rich in protein, calcium, iron, potassium, manganese, and vitamins (A, B, and D), and is a good source of fiber.

MAIN MEALS

You would be surprised how many everyday foods are already gluten-free and vegan. Here I will show you how to simply convert a variety of your favorite main dishes into delicious gluten-free and vegan. I used a lot of whole foods, simple sauces made from scratch.

My first time hearing about African peanut stew, or groundnut stew, was while I was in college. My classmate would reminisce about this delicious stew she would eat in her country. I often wondered how would ground peanut taste in a stew. My culinary taste buds were at that time limited to Caribbean, Indian, Chinese, and British cuisine, and although I was open to try dishes from other cultures, I couldn't fathom that it would taste desirable. Many years later, I experimented with this stew, and what a treat it was. I was very impressed with the results.

DIRECTIONS:

Sort and wash split peas and place in a large pot along with water. Bring to boil on medium heat, cover pot and lower to simmer. Cook for 40 minutes until peas are soft. Add onion, garlic, ginger, tomatoes and sweet potatoes. Cook for 10-15 minutes until potatoes are tender. Remove 1 cup of liquid and mix with peanut butter to form a thick sauce, return to pot along with tomato sauce, collard greens and salt. Cook for 5 minutes, stirring constantly for flavors to blend.

INGREDIENTS:

1 cup (150g) green split peas
4 cups (960ml) vegetable stock or water
1 medium onion, chopped
2 cloves garlic, minced
2 tablespoons freshly grated ginger
2 large tomatoes, diced
1 cup (133g) sweet potatoes, chopped
1 cup (244g) tomato sauce
½ cup (129g) peanut butter
½ cup (33g) collard greens leafs or kale, roughly chopped
1 ½ teaspoon sea salt or to taste

These tofu nuggets are a winner in my home. My children love them with homemade barbecue sauce or ketchup. They are great for the picky eaters. You can also freeze, then defrost the tofu before preparing for a more chewy texture. I usually omit this process because I use a very firm tofu, but you might want to include this step if your tofu is on the softer side.

INGREDIENTS:

1 pound (454g) extra firm tofu
2 tablespoons Bragg's liquid aminos or soy sauce
2 tablespoons nutritional yeast flakes
2 tablespoons brown rice flour
1 teaspoon dried onion
½ teaspoon dried garlic
¼ teaspoon ground sage
¼ teaspoon marjoram
¼ teaspoon paprika
Pinch ground rosemary
Pinch dried thyme
Pinch Cayenne pepper (optional)
½ cup (122g) barbecue sauce, ketchup or salsa

DIRECTIONS:

Press tofu between paper towels to remove excess water. Then cut in strips or cubes and marinate with liquid aminos, then set aside for 20 minutes. Preheat oven 400°F/200°C.

In another bowl, combine the remaining ingredients well. Coat tofu with dry mix and place on a greased baking sheet. Bake for approximately 30 minutes, turning halfway. You may also cook on a lightly oiled frying pan until golden and crispy. Serve with your favorite barbecue sauce, ketchup or salsa.

Chef's Tip: You can add tofu nuggets to fried rice or any of the side dishes to create one pot dishes.

Cauliflower is a member of the cruciferous family, it contains antioxidants and plant chemicals that protects from cancer. It is high in fiber so it lets you feel full for longer, assists in weight loss and is great for bowel health. Feel free to substitute your favorite barbecue sauce in this recipe instead.

INGREDIENTS:

1 head cauliflower, cut into florets
1/3 cup (45g) brown rice flour
2/3 cup (75ml) almond milk
2 tablespoons almond butter
1 teaspoon sea salt
Barbecue Sauce
2 teaspoons olive oil or 2 tablespoons water
2 tablespoons onion, minced
2 cloves garlic, minced
1 ½ cups (366g) tomato sauce
2 tablespoons maple syrup
1 teaspoon molasses
½ teaspoon cumin
½ teaspoon parsley
¼ teaspoon Cayenne pepper
½ teaspoon sea salt

DIRECTIONS:

Preheat oven 450°F/230°C. Lightly grease baking sheet lined with parchment paper. In a large bowl, combine brown rice flour, almond butter, milk, and salt to form a batter. Add cauliflower florets and toss well. Spread in single layer on baking sheet. Bake for 15 minutes, turn and bake for 5 minutes.

To make the barbecue sauce: Heat oil or water in a medium saucepan on medium-high heat. Cook onion until soft, about 4 minutes. Add garlic and cook for 30 seconds. Add tomato sauce, maple syrup, molasses, cumin, parsley, Cayenne pepper and salt. Bring to boil, reduce heat to a simmer for 10 minutes or until sauce is thickened.

Coat each cauliflower floret with barbecue sauce, return to oven and bake for 5-10 minutes or until cauliflower is crispy. Serve with vegetable crudités and your favorite dip.

I share this dish in loving memory of a dear friend, Barbara Raimey, who taught me how to make barbecue tofu. I have cooked this dish more than any other and it is always a winner. Barbara came to visit our family several times. She was quiet and sweet and didn't say too much. She would love to visit because I lived in the countryside, where it was peaceful and quiet. While she stayed with our family, she didn't ask for much; she was content and happy and enjoyed just being with us. She would spend hours walking with Devannah and me when Devannah was 6 years old. At the time, I didn't know Barbara had terminal cancer. I found out that at one point she was an owner of a vegan restaurant and had years of experience as a chef.

INGREDIENTS:

Batter
1 pound (454g) extra firm tofu, drained and pressed
¼ cup (64g) creamy peanut butter or tahini paste
1 tablespoon olive oil
1 teaspoon onion powder
½ teaspoon garlic powder
1 teaspoon nutritional yeast flakes (optional)
½ teaspoon sea salt
Pinch cumin

Barbecue Sauce
2 teaspoons olive oil or 2 tablespoons water
¼ cup (40g) minced onion
1 clove garlic
28 ounces (794g) tomato puree or sauce
¼ cup (60ml) maple syrup
2 tablespoons coconut palm sugar
1 tablespoon pomegranate molasses
1 tablespoon parsley flakes
2 tablespoons Bragg's liquid aminos or coconut aminos
¼ teaspoon sesame oil (optional)
Sea salt to taste

DIRECTIONS:

For barbecue sauce: In a medium saucepan, heat oil or water on medium heat. Add onion and cook until soft, about 4 minutes. Stir in garlic and cook for 30 seconds. Add tomato sauce, maple syrup, coconut palm sugar, molasses, parsley, Bragg's liquid aminos, sesame oil and sea salt to taste. Reduce heat to simmer for 15–20 minutes, stirring constantly until sauce is thickened.

For Tofu: Preheat oven 400°F/200°C. Drain water from tofu and squeezed excess water out between paper towels or a clean dishcloth. Cut tofu in long strips and set aside. Combine batter in a bowl and mix well. Coat individual tofu strips with batter mix and place on an oiled 9x13 casserole dish. Bake tofu for 20 minutes, or until tofu is golden brown.

Evenly coat tofu with barbecue sauce and return to the oven for 5-10 minutes.

Chef's Tip: Unsulphured molasses can be used as substitute for pomegranate molasses

Cashew Gravy

½ cup (62g) raw cashews, washed and soaked for at least 4 hours

2 cups (480ml) water

2 tablespoons onion, chopped

1 clove garlic

1 tablespoon arrowroot powder

1 tablespoon nutritional yeast flakes

¼ teaspoon rosemary

¼ teaspoon thyme

Pinch of sage

Pinch of allspice (optional)

½ teaspoon sea salt

Beets' earthy and sweet flavor blends well with black beans along with earthy spices of cumin, oregano and thyme to make these delicious beet balls. This is a great way to use beets and another winner recipe to serve to picky eaters. It is delicious served with cashew gravy or brown rice gravy.

INGREDIENTS:

2 medium beets, scrubbed, ends trimmed, and cut in quarters

2 tablespoons olive oil, divided

1½ cups cooked or 1 (15- ounce/425g) can black beans, drained and rinsed

1 cup (160g) onion, finely minced

3 cloves garlic, minced

1 teaspoon dried parsley

½ teaspoon cumin

½ teaspoon dried oregano

¼ teaspoon dried thyme

½ cup (60g) oat flour

½ cup (50g) walnut, finely chopped

2 tablespoons Bragg's liquid aminos

2 tablespoons nutritional yeast flakes

DIRECTIONS:

Beet Balls: Preheat oven 400°F/200°C. Toss beets and 1 tablespoon of olive oil in a bowl. Spread in a single layer on a greased baking sheet and roast for 45 minutes. Allow beets to cool for 10 minutes. Peel beets and place food processor with black beans; process just enough to combine. Transfer to a bowl and set aside.

Heat remaining 1 tablespoon olive oil in a skillet on medium heat, add onion and cook until soft, about 4 minutes. Stir in garlic and cook for 30 seconds. Add to beet/black bean mixture with cumin, oregano, thyme, oat flour, walnuts, liquid aminos and yeast flakes to combine. Shape into balls and place on a baking sheet in a single layer. Bake for 30 minutes, turning the balls over after 15 minutes. Serve with cashew gravy.

Cashew Gravy: Place cashews, water, and remaining ingredients in a blender and process until smooth. Transfer to a saucepan on medium heat, whisking constantly until thickened, about 2 minutes.

This dish is rich and flavorful, packed full of colorful vegetables, black beans, corn and red bell peppers. I used brown rice tortillas for this recipe, but you can use your own favorite tortilla.

INGREDIENTS:

Enchilada Sauce
1 tablespoon olive oil or ¼ cup water
1 small onion, chopped
2 cloves garlic, minced
½ teaspoon oregano
1 ½ teaspoon chili powder
1 teaspoon cumin
1 tablespoon brown rice flour
1 tablespoon coconut palm sugar
1½ cups (366g) tomato sauce
1 cup (60 ml) water
1 teaspoon sea salt

Filling
1 tablespoon olive oil or ¼ cup water
2 cloves garlic, minced
1 small onion, minced
¼ cup (39g) chopped red bell pepper
3 cups cooked black beans or 2 (15-ounce/425g) cans drained and rinsed
1 cup (125g) corn kernels
½ teaspoon cumin
¼ cup (4g) cilantro, chopped
¼ teaspoon oregano
¼ teaspoon sea salt

Cashew Sauce
1½ cup (167g) raw cashews, soaked for at least 4 hours
¾ cup (180ml) water
½ cup (58g) red bell pepper, chopped
2 tablespoons onion
1 clove garlic
2 tablespoons nutritional yeast flakes
1 tablespoon tapioca starch
1 teaspoon sea salt
Chopped avocados, bell peppers and cilantro leaves for garnish
8 brown rice or corn tortillas

58

DIRECTIONS:

Preheat oven 350°F/175°C. Heat oil or water in a saucepan over medium heat, add onions and cook until soft, about 4 minutes. Add garlic and cook for 30 seconds. Add oregano, chili powder, cumin, brown rice flour, and coconut palm sugar, stirring for a minute. Add tomato sauce, water and salt, and allow to simmer for about 5 minutes. Transfer sauce to blender and process until smooth.

To prepare black beans: Heat oil or water in medium saucepan on medium high heat. Add onions and cook until soft. Add garlic and cook for 30 seconds. Stir in black beans, corn kernels, red bell pepper, cumin, cilantro and oregano. Lower heat and simmer for 3-5 minutes.

Cashew Sauce: In a blender, combine cashews with water and process until smooth. Add red bell pepper, onion, garlic, nutritional yeast flakes, tapioca starch and sea salt. Continue processing until sauce is smooth.

Prepare tortillas: Heat a dry skillet on medium high heat. Add tortilla and cook on each side for a couple of seconds, one at a time, until the remaining tortillas are cooked. Cover on a plate until ready.

Assemble Enchiladas: In an oiled 9x13 casserole dish, spread a thin layer of enchilada sauce. Add about ¼ cup of bean filling and 1 tablespoon of cashew sauce into the center of a tortilla. Roll up tightly and place seam side down. Pour remaining black beans over enchiladas, followed by enchilada sauce and cashew sauce. Bake for 25-30 minutes uncovered. Serve garnished with chopped avocado, red bell pepper and cilantro leaves.

BLACKBEAN QUINOA BURRITO BOWL

This protein packed bowl is super easy to make, delicious, and light, yet it's very satisfying. Be creative and use your favorite vegetables in this recipe.

INGREDIENTS:

Quinoa
1 cup (184g) quinoa
2 cups (480ml) water
Pinch of sea salt

Sweet Potato
1 medium sweet potato, peeled and chopped
1 tablespoon coconut oil

Seasoned Black Beans
1 tablespoon coconut oil or ¼ cup water
½ cup(80g) onion, finely chopped
2 cloves garlic, minced
1 ½ cups cooked or 1 (15-ounce/425g) can black beans
¼ teaspoon oregano
2 sprigs of thyme
Sea salt to taste
Pinch of Cayenne pepper
1 cup (125g) sweet corn kernels
1 avocado, chopped
1 cup (140g) grape tomatoes, halved

Cilantro Lime Dressing
½ cup (62g) raw cashews, rinsed and drained
½ cup (120ml) water
½ cup (8g) cilantro
1 tablespoon lime juice
1 tablespoon onion, chopped
1 tablespoon nutritional yeast flakes
1 clove garlic
½ teaspoon sea salt

DIRECTIONS:

Rinse quinoa using a fine mesh sieve, place into a saucepan with water and salt on medium heat. Bring to boil, reduce to simmer and cover pot. Cook for 20 minutes or until tender. Fluff quinoa with fork and set aside.

Preheat oven on 400°F/200°C. Grease baking sheet and set aside. Toss sweet potatoes with oil and spread on baking sheet. Roast for about 20 minutes or until golden brown.

To cook beans: Heat oil or water on medium high heat. Add onion and cook until soft. Stir in garlic and cook for 30 seconds. Add black beans, oregano, thyme, salt and Cayenne pepper. Cook until beans are warm through, stirring often.

For Dressing: Place cashews and water in a high speed blender and process until smooth. Add cilantro, nutritional yeast flakes, lime juice, onion, garlic and sea salt and continue processing. May need to add extra water to get desired consistency.

To Serve: Arrange quinoa, sweet potato, black beans, corn, avocado and tomatoes in a bowl along with cilantro lime dressing.

Scrumptious shredded cabbage, seasoned with spicy aromatics, formed into balls and baked instead of fried. Then served in a spicy and flavorful gravy.

INGREDIENTS:

For the cabbage balls:
2 cups (198g) cabbage, finely shredded
1 tablespoon coconut oil
¼ cup (40g) onion, finely minced
1 clove garlic, minced
¼ teaspoon coriander
¼ teaspoon cumin
½ teaspoon sea salt
¼ cup (30g) chickpea/garbanzo flour

Curry Sauce
1 tablespoon coconut oil or ¼ cup water
1 onion, minced
2 cloves garlic, minced
1 teaspoon ginger, grated
1 medium tomato, chopped
½ teaspoon coriander
¼ teaspoon turmeric
¼ teaspoon cumin
2 tablespoons chickpea/garbanzo flour
1 cup (240ml) coconut milk
1 cup (240ml) water
1 bay leaf

¼ teaspoon Cayenne pepper (optional)
1 teaspoon sea salt
2 tablespoons cilantro leaves, plus extra for garnishing

DIRECTIONS:

To make cabbage balls: Place cabbage in a food processor and pulse until finely shredded. Transfer shredded cabbage into a bowl and set aside.

Preheat oven 400°F/200°C. Lightly grease a baking sheet and set aside. Heat oil in a skillet on medium heat, add onion, garlic and cook until onion is soft. Stir in coriander, cumin and cook for another minute. Add shredded cabbage and cook, while stirring, for about 5 minutes, or until cabbage is tender. Season with salt to taste. Transfer cabbage into a bowl and allow to cool. Stir in chickpea flour and mix well to form a smooth dough. Shape cabbage dough into equal sized balls. Transfer onto baking sheet and bake for 30 minutes, turning after 15 minutes.

To make sauce: Heat oil or water in a large saucepan on medium heat, add onion and cook until soft, about 4 minutes. Add garlic and ginger, cook for about 1 minute. Stir in tomatoes and cook for another 2 minutes. Add coriander, turmeric, cumin and chickpea flour, stirring constantly for about 1 minute. Stir into saucepan, coconut milk, water, bay leaf, Cayenne and salt to taste. Cover saucepan and bring to a boil. Reduce to simmer for about 10 minutes, or until the sauce thickens. Turn off heat and stir in cilantro leaves. Add cabbage balls and serve over rice or potatoes.

CHICKPEAS AND DUMPLINGS

This comforting stew is my version of the popular Southern dish, chicken and dumplings. I used chickpeas as the protein, cooked in a creamy vegetable stew and topped with gluten-free dumplings.

INGREDIENTS:

1 tablespoons olive oil or ¼ cup (60ml) water
1 medium onion, finely chopped
3 cloves garlic, minced
2 stalks celery chopped
1 carrot, cut into circles
1 medium potato, diced
4 sprigs of thyme
1 tablespoon fresh parsley, chopped
¾ teaspoon rubbed sage
1 tablespoon nutritional yeast flakes
1 ½ cups cooked or 1 (15- ounce/425g) can chickpeas
1 tablespoon Bragg's liquid aminos
3 cups (720g) water or vegetable broth
1 bay leaf
¾ teaspoon sea salt

Dumplings

1 tablespoon ground golden flax seeds
¼ cup (60ml) water or almond milk
½ cup (70g) brown rice flour
½ cup (50g) corn flour
2 tablespoons tapioca starch
2 tablespoons potato starch
¼ teaspoon baking powder
1 finely chopped spring onion (white part only)
1 tablespoon fresh parsley, minced
½ teaspoon fresh thyme leaves, minced
¼ teaspoon sea salt
¼ cup (60ml) almond milk

DIRECTIONS:

Heat oil or water in a large saucepan on medium heat. Add onion and cook until soft, about 4 minutes. Add garlic and cook for 30 seconds. Add celery, carrots, potatoes, thyme, parsley, sage and yeast flakes stirring to coat. Add chickpeas, liquid aminos, water and bay leaf. Cover saucepan and bring to a boil. Reduce to a simmer and cook for about 20 minutes. Add salt to taste.

To make dumplings: Stir flax seeds and almond milk in a small bowl, and set aside for 3 minutes. In a medium bowl, combine brown rice flour, tapioca starch, potato starch, baking powder, onion, parsley thyme leaves and sea salt. Combine flax seed mixture and remaining almond milk. Add to the flour mixture and knead to form a dough. Drop heaping tablespoons on top of chickpeas. Cover and cook until dumplings are fully cooked, around 12 minutes.

This richly-flavored stew highlights cauliflower and chickpeas, cooked in aromatic spices and creamy coconut milk.

INGREDIENTS:

1 tablespoon coconut oil or ¼ cup (60ml) water
1 medium onion, finely chopped
4 cloves garlic, minced
1 tablespoon grated fresh ginger
1 teaspoon ground turmeric
1 teaspoon ground coriander
½ teaspoon ground cumin
4 cups (400g) cauliflower florets
2 medium carrots, sliced
1 ½ cups cooked or 1 (15-ounce/425g) can chickpeas, drained and rinsed
1 cup (110g) frozen peas, thawed
1 (14-ounce /400g) can coconut milk
1 cup (240ml) water
2 sprigs of thyme
1 teaspoon sea salt
¼ cup (4g) cilantro, chopped
Hot cooked rice to serve

DIRECTIONS:

Heat the oil or water in a large saucepan over medium high heat. Add onion and cook until soft. Stir in garlic and ginger and cook for 1 minute. Add turmeric, coriander, cumin and cook, stirring for 30 seconds. Add cauliflower florets, carrots, chickpeas and stir to coat with seasonings. Add coconut milk, water and thyme. Cover saucepan and bring to a boil. Reduce to a simmer and cook for about 20 minutes, or until cauliflower is tender. Stir in frozen peas and cilantro and season with salt to taste. Serve over hot rice.

CAULIFLOWER FRIED RICE

YIELD: 4 SERVINGS

Cauliflower fried rice is one of the most popular recipes on my website, so I decided to include another version in my cookbook. I added some peanut butter along with the sesame oil for this delicious Asian style treat.

INGREDIENTS:

1 head cauliflower
1 tablespoon of coconut oil or ¼ cup water
1 onion, finely chopped
3 cloves garlic, chopped
1 tablespoon ginger, minced
1 carrot, chopped
½ cup (62g) corn kernels
½ cup (55g) green peas
1 tablespoon sesame oil
¼ cup (60ml) Bragg's liquid aminos
2 tablespoons coconut palm sugar
1 tablespoon peanut butter
2 sliced green onions (white and green parts)

DIRECTIONS:

Break cauliflower into small florets. Using a food processor, pulse batches of florets into small rice-like grains. Heat oil or water in a large skillet on medium high heat. Add onion and cook until soft. Stir in garlic and ginger, and cook for 1 minute. Add cauliflower rice and cook for 3 minutes, constantly stirring. Add carrots, corn, and green peas, and cook for 3 more minutes. Combine sesame oil, liquid aminos, coconut palm sugar, and peanut butter in a small bowl. Stir mixture into cauliflower rice, cover and cook for 3 more minutes until tender. Stir in green onions and serve.

Chef's Tip: Use the coarse side of a large grater if you don't have a food processor.

A couple years ago, I catered for a Jewish gathering, and chickpea balls were one of the dishes that I prepared that got rave reviews from the guests. Chickpeas are mashed and seasoned with Italian herbs, then I made a tomato/coconut-based sauce with Indian spices. The resulting dish is bursting with flavors.

INGREDIENTS:

2 tablespoons ground flax seeds or chia seeds
3 tablespoon water
1 tablespoon olive oil or ¼ cup water
1 onion, finely chopped
2 garlic cloves, minced
1 ½ cups cooked or (1 15-ounce/425g) can chickpeas, drained
1 cup (112g) almond flour
½ teaspoon oregano
½ teaspoon basil
½ teaspoon parsley
½ teaspoon sea salt

Sauce
2 teaspoon olive oil or ¼ cup (60ml) water
1 onion, chopped
4 cloves garlic, minced
½ inch ginger, grated
4 medium tomatoes, chopped
1 teaspoon coriander
¼ teaspoon turmeric
½ teaspoon sea salt
Pinch of fennel seeds (optional)
2 tablespoons coconut milk
½ cup (122g) marinara sauce

DIRECTIONS:

To make Chickpea Balls: Preheat oven 400°F/200°C. Lightly oil baking sheet and set aside. Combine flax seed and water in a small bowl and set aside for 3 minutes. In a small skillet, sauté onion and garlic until soft. In a large bowl, add mashed chickpeas, almond flour, flax seed mix, onion, garlic, oregano, basil, parsley and salt. Using both hands, form into balls and bake for 30 minutes, turning halfway.

To Make Sauce: Heat oil or water in a large saucepan on medium-high heat. Add onion and cook until soft. Stir in garlic and ginger and cook for 1 minute. Add tomatoes and continue to cook for 2 minutes. Add turmeric, coriander, fennel, coconut milk and marinara sauce. Cover and bring to boil, then reduce to a simmer. Cook for 10 minutes, then season with salt to taste.

I made these patties because of my love for falafel. Falafel is a Middle Eastern dish that is made with pureed chickpeas and or fava beans, then is seasoned, formed into balls and deep fried. They are then served in a pita bread and topped with vegetables, pickles and a tahini-based sauce. In this version, I added carrots, formed into patties, and baked instead of deep frying. I also made a vegan tahini sauce for serving.

INGREDIENTS:

1 ½ cups cooked or (15 ounces/425g) can chickpeas, drained and mashed
1 medium carrot, grated
1 cup (160g) onion, chopped
4 cloves garlic, minced
2 tablespoons fresh parsley, chopped
¼ cup (4g) cilantro, chopped, plus extra for garnish
¼ teaspoon smoked paprika
¼ teaspoon cumin
2 tablespoons sesame tahini paste
2 tablespoons lemon juice
3 tablespoons chickpea/garbanzo flour
¼ teaspoon Cayenne pepper (optional)
½ teaspoon sea salt or to taste

Tahini Dressing
¼ cup (56g) tahini paste
¼ cup (60ml) water
1 tablespoon lemon juice
1 tablespoon olive oil
1 teaspoon maple syrup (optional)
½ teaspoon sea salt (or to taste)

DIRECTIONS:

Preheat oven 400°F/200°C. In a large bowl, add chickpeas and mash with a fork. Add all the remaining ingredients and mix very well. Form into patties and place on prepared baking sheet. Bake for 30 minutes, turning halfway. It is delicious in gluten-free pita bread, with tahini dressing and chopped cilantro.

Tahini Dressing: Whisk or blend ingredients together, and add additional water depending on desired thickness.

Thick slices of eggplant are dipped into flax seed gel, followed by seasoned gluten-free breading. They are baked to the perfect crispness. Served topped with marinara sauce and cashew cheese sauce.

INGREDIENTS:

2 tablespoons ground flax seeds or chia seeds
1 cup (60ml) water
1 large eggplant cut in slices
½ cup (70g) brown rice flour
¼ cup (12g) nutritional yeast flakes
1 teaspoon onion powder
½ teaspoon garlic powder
½ teaspoon paprika
1 teaspoon sea salt
½ teaspoon Italian seasoning
Cayenne pepper (optional)
Marinara sauce
Cheesy Cashew Basil Sauce
1 cup (125g) raw cashews
½ cup (120ml) water
2 tablespoons nutritional yeast flakes
1 tablespoon chopped onion
1 clove garlic, chopped
2 teaspoons tapioca starch
½ teaspoon dried basil
½ teaspoon sea salt

DIRECTIONS:

Wash and slice eggplant into ¼ inch slices, sprinkle with sea salt and set aside in a bowl for 20 minutes. Make flax seed gel by mixing flax seed and water in a saucepan, bring to boil and simmer for 10 minutes, stirring until a gel is formed. Remove from the stove and strain into a shallow bowl to cool. Combine brown rice flour, nutritional yeast flakes, onion powder, garlic powder, paprika, sea salt and Italian seasoning in a bowl.

Rinse and dry eggplant slice, dip each slice into flax seed gel, then into the seasoning mix. Place on a greased baking sheet, bake at 425°F/220°C for 30 minutes, turning after 15 minutes. Top with marinara sauce and cheesy cashew basil sauce and serve over gluten-free pasta.

GREEN JACKFRUIT CURRY

This is one of my favorite dishes to make for my guests. The meat-like texture of the green jackfruit raises a lot of curiosity when served to someone who isn't familiar with it. I recommend you use fresh or canned; I don't like the flavor and texture of the frozen ones I have tried. The jackfruit was not fully green and the texture was softer than that of the others.

INGREDIENTS:

1 tablespoon coconut oil or ¼ cup (60ml) water
1 onion, chopped
4 cloves garlic, minced
1 inch ginger root
1 ½ teaspoons coriander
1 teaspoon turmeric
1 teaspoon cumin
½ teaspoon dried thyme
¼ teaspoon ground fennel
1 medium tomato, chopped
4 medium potatoes, chopped
1 (20-ounce/480g) green jackfruit
1 can (14-ounce/400ml) coconut milk
1 cup (24ml) water
1 teaspoon sea salt
Pinch Cayenne pepper (optional)

DIRECTIONS:

Heat a large saucepan with oil. Add onion and cook until soft. Stir in garlic and ginger, cook for 30 seconds. Add coriander, turmeric, cumin, thyme, fennel and cook for 1 minute, stirring constantly. Add tomatoes, potatoes, jackfruit, and cook, stirring to coat for 2 minutes. Add coconut milk and water, cover saucepan and bring to a boil. Reduce heat and simmer for 25-30 minutes or until sauce is thick. Season with salt and serve with brown rice or quinoa.

This is a very quick and easy meal to prepare. Jamaican pumpkins can be purchased at international food stores. Substitute acorn or butternut squash for an equally flavorful dish.

INGREDIENTS:

2 pounds (0.90 kilo) pumpkin cut into cubes
1 tablespoon coconut oil or ¼ (60ml) cup water
1 medium onion, chopped
4 cloves garlic, minced
1 inch ginger, grated
1 medium tomato, chopped
2 tablespoons curry powder
1 (14-ounce/400ml) can coconut milk
1 cup (240ml) water
2 sprigs of thyme
1 whole Scotch Bonnet pepper (optional)
1 teaspoon sea salt or to taste

DIRECTIONS:

Heat oil or water in large saucepan, add onion, and sauté until translucent, or about 3 minutes. Stir in garlic, ginger, tomato and curry powder, cook for another minute. Stir in pumpkin, coconut milk, water, and thyme, and bring to simmer. Add pepper and cook on low until pumpkin is tender and sauce is thickened (about 30 minutes). Add salt and serve.

Gumbo is the official state dish of Louisiana. The name gumbo is derived from a West African word for okra, 'gombo'. The dish is rooted in Creole and Cajun cooking. It is a flavorful dark roux stew consisting of meat or shellfish, okra and/or file powder, and vegetables, including tomatoes and onion, served with rice. This version is made with kidney beans. I decided not to use the roux method, but I added the okra instead, which was enough to thicken the stew.

INGREDIENTS:

1 tablespoon olive oil or ¼ cup water
1 medium onion, chopped
4 cloves garlic, minced
1 red bell pepper, diced
1 cup (140g) tomatoes, chopped
1 cup (100g) fresh or frozen okra
½ teaspoon dried thyme
½ teaspoon oregano
½ teaspoon cumin
½ teaspoon coriander
¼ teaspoon smoked paprika
1 (28 -ounce/794g) crushed tomatoes
1 tablespoon Bragg's liquid aminos
2 chopped green onions (white and green parts)
3 cups cooked or 2 (15- ounce/425g) can kidney beans

3 cups (720ml) water or vegetable stock
2 bay leaves
1 teaspoon sea salt or to taste
¼ teaspoon Cayenne pepper (optional)

DIRECTIONS:

Heat oil or water in a large pot on medium heat. Add onion and cook until soft. Stir in garlic and cook for 30 seconds. Add bell pepper, tomatoes, and okra, and continue to cook, stirring for 3 minutes. Next, add thyme, oregano, cumin, coriander, and paprika. Stir in crushed tomatoes, liquid aminos, green onions, kidney beans, water, and bay leaves. Bring gumbo to a boil and reduce heat to simmer. Cook for 20 minutes. Add salt and Cayenne pepper to taste. It is delicious served with brown rice.

Looking for delicious comfort food?. Look no further. This delicious lentil rice loaf is perfect to take the centerpiece of your holiday table. Use green or brown lentils instead of red lentils.

INGREDIENTS:

1 cup (150g) dry lentils
2 cups (240ml) water
1 tablespoon olive oil
1/2 medium onion, finely minced
2 cloves garlic, minced
1 celery stalk, finely chopped
1 medium carrot, shredded
1 teaspoon dried thyme
1 teaspoon dried parsley flakes
2 cups (280g) cooked brown rice
2 tablespoons Bragg's liquid aminos
1/4 cup (26g) flax seed meal
1/2 cup (60g) walnuts, chopped
1/2 teaspoon sea salt
1/4 cup (60ml) barbecue sauce or ketchup

DIRECTIONS:

Sort, wash and drain lentils using a fine mesh strainer. Place into a medium pot with cold water, bring to boil on medium high. Reduce heat to a simmer and cook for 45 minutes or until lentils are tender and water has evaporated. Transfer lentil to a large bowl, mash using fork and set aside.

Preheat oven 375°F/190°C. Line 9 (23cm) x 5 (13cm) inches loaf pan with parchment paper and set aside. Heat oil on medium high heat in a large saucepan. Add onion and saute for 4 minutes until soft. Stir in garlic, celery, carrot , thyme, parsley and cook for 4 minutes, stirring constantly. Stir in brown rice and liquid aminos until coated with vegetables, about 1 minute. Transfer rice mixture to lentil and add flax seed meal, walnuts and salt. Mix to thoroughly to blend, spoon lentil/rice mixture and gently press down into prepared pan.

Spread barbecue sauce or ketchup on top and bake for 45 minutes uncovered. Cool for 10 minutes in pan, then transfer to serving platter. Delicious served with roasted potatoes, garnish with fresh parsley.

This is a freshly made lentil stew, enhanced by the earthy flavors of cumin, oregano, thyme and all-spice. You won't even miss the meat.

INGREDIENTS:

1 tablespoon olive oil or ¼ cup water
1 medium onion, minced
2 cloves garlic, minced
1 cup (150g) dried lentils, rinsed
3 cups (720ml) water or vegetable broth
½ teaspoon cumin
½ teaspoon paprika
½ teaspoon oregano
2 sprigs thyme
1 chopped green onion (white and green parts)
1 teaspoon nutritional yeast flakes (optional)
Pinch allspice powder
½ teaspoon sea salt or to taste
Pinch Cayenne pepper

DIRECTIONS:

Heat oil or water in a medium pot on medium-high heat. Add onion and cook until soft. Add garlic and cook for 30 seconds. Stir in lentils, cumin, paprika, oregano, thyme, green onions, nutritional yeast flakes, allspice, and water or vegetable broth. Cover pot and bring to boil, then reduce to simmer and cook for 30 minutes, until lentils are tender. Serve with rice.

Lentil tacos are healthy, and you don't even miss the meat in this recipe. This is another dish that you can serve to picky eaters. The smoky flavor of the lentil blends well with the spicy aromatics in this hearty taco filling.

INGREDIENTS:

1 tablespoon olive oil or ¼ cup water
1 onion, minced
2 cloves garlic, minced
1 cup (150g) dried lentils, rinsed
3 cups (720ml) water or vegetable broth
½ teaspoon cumin
½ teaspoon paprika
½ teaspoon oregano
2 sprigs thyme
1 chopped green onion (white and green parts)
1 teaspoons nutritional yeast flakes (optional)
Pinch allspice powder
½ teaspoon sea salt or to taste
Pinch Cayenne pepper
8 taco shells
1 cup (47g) lettuce, shredded
1 cup (112g) vegan shredded cheese
1 cup (140g) tomato, chopped

DIRECTIONS:

Heat oil or water in a medium pot on medium-high heat. Add onion and cook until soft. Add garlic and cook for 30 seconds. Stir in lentils, cumin, paprika, oregano, thyme, green onions, nutritional yeast flakes, allspice, and water or vegetable broth. Cover pot and bring to boil, then reduce to simmer and cook for 30 minutes, or until lentils are tender. Uncover pot and let remaining liquid evaporate. Mash lentils with a fork. To serve, spoon lentils in taco shells, top with lettuce, tomato and cheese.

Chef's Tip: Make sure to use the green or brown lentils in this recipe.

73

LIMA BEAN STEW

YIELD: 8 SERVINGS

This dish is very comforting, especially during the cold season or on a rainy day. It is very flavorful and goes well served with rice.

INGREDIENTS:

1 pound (474g) dried baby lima beans,
6 cups (1.4 Liter) water
1 tablespoon olive oil or ¼ cup water
1 medium onion, chopped
3 cloves garlic, minced
½ inch ginger, grated
1 teaspoon dried thyme
1 teaspoon turmeric
1 teaspoon coriander
½ teaspoon cumin
2 medium carrots, chopped
1 medium potato, peeled and chopped
1 bay leaf
1 teaspoon sea salt or to taste

DIRECTIONS:

Sort beans, then rinse and soak beans overnight or use the quick cook method, which is covering beans with about 2 inches of water above beans, bringing to boil for 5 minutes, then cover and leave for 2 hours. Drain and set aside.

Heat oil or water in a large pot and sauté onions for about 3 minutes until softened. Add garlic and ginger cooking for another minute. Stir in thyme, turmeric, coriander, and cumin. Add potatoes and carrots and continue to stir, coating vegetables. Add water, beans and bay leaf. Bring to a boil, cover partially, and reduce heat to low. Simmer for 45 minutes, until beans are tender and creamy. Remove bay leaf and season with salt to taste. Serve with brown rice, quinoa or millet.

SWEET POTATO & CAULIFLOWER MAC N' CHEESE

YIELD: 4 SERVINGS

This creamy macaroni and cheese recipe is packed full with nutrients with the addition of sweet potato and cauliflower. The bright orange color gives the appearance that a lot of processed cheese has been added. This recipe is a great way to incorporate vegetables into this ultimate comfort food without the use of butter, flour, or cheese.

INGREDIENTS:

8 ounce (227g) package of gluten-free elbow macaroni pasta
1 cup (133g) sweet potato, chopped
1 cup (100g) cauliflower florets
¼ cup (12g) nutritional yeast flakes
¼ cup (60ml) almond milk
1 tablespoon onion, chopped
2 cloves garlic
1 ½ teaspoon sea salt

DIRECTIONS:

Bring a large pot of water to boil, then add pasta and cook according to package directions. Drain pasta and return to the pot.

In another large pot, steam sweet potato and cauliflower until tender, or about 15 minutes. Drain sweet potato and cauliflower florets. Place sweet potato, cauliflower, yeast flakes, almond milk, onion, garlic and salt in a high speed blender, and process until smooth. Add sauce to pasta and stir well to coat. Serve hot.

This is a delicious take on the popular Chinese take-out dish. Ditch take-out with the added MSG (monosodium glutamate), and make this delicious dish. MSG is a flavor enhancer that is frequently added to Chinese foods and other processed foods. These are some of the symptoms that have been reported: headache, numbness and tingling in the face and other areas, chest pains, heart palpitations, and nausea.

INGREDIENTS:

1 pound (474g) block of extra firm tofu, pressed and cut into cubes
1 tablespoon water
½ cup (120ml) orange juice
1 tablespoon arrowroot
4 tablespoons Bragg's liquid aminos
3 tablespoons coconut palm sugar
2 cloves garlic, minced
1 ½ tablespoons fresh ginger, grated
1 tablespoon olive oil
¼ teaspoon sesame oil
1 sliced green onion (white and green parts)

DIRECTIONS:

In a baking dish, add tofu cubes and set aside. In a smaller bowl, whisk water, orange juice, arrowroot, liquid aminos, coconut palm sugar, garlic, ginger, olive oil and sesame oil. Pour marinade over tofu and allow to marinate for at least 4 hours or overnight in the refrigerator. Pour off the marinade in a small saucepan and transfer the tofu to a lightly greased baking sheet and bake in a preheated oven at 400°F/200°C for 30 minutes, turning after 15 minutes. Bring the reserved marinade to a boil on medium heat, stirring constantly with a whisk until thicken. Reduce heat and add green onion. Add to tofu. Serve with brown rice.

SESAME GINGER SOY CURLS

Soy curls are another versatile meat alternative. They are certified GMO-free and grown without chemical pesticides. The whole beans are cooked in spring water, then stirred while being cooked. They are mashed and dried using low temperatures. Basically, they are not made from isolated proteins, but are whole organic soybeans.

INGREDIENTS:

Baked soy curls
2 cups (80g) Butler's soy curls
2 tablespoons nutritional yeast flakes
2 tablespoons Bragg's liquid aminos
1 teaspoon parsley
2 tablespoons tapioca starch
Sauce
¼ cup (60ml) water
¼ cup (60ml) Bragg's liquid aminos
¼ cup (48g) coconut palm sugar
1 tablespoon lemon juice
1 teaspoon sesame oil
1 tablespoon tapioca starch
1 tablespoon coconut oil or ¼ cup water
1 onion, chopped
2 cloves garlic, minced
1 inch ginger, finely chopped
1 red bell pepper, cut into strips
1 chopped green onion (green parts) for garnish

DIRECTIONS:

Preheat oven 400°F/200°C. Prepare baking sheet with lightly greased parchment paper and set aside. Place soy curls in a bowl and cover with warm water to rehydrate for about 10 minutes, and then drain. Combine soy curls with yeast flakes, liquid aminos, parsley, and tapioca starch. Place soy curls in a single layer on baking sheet and bake for 20 minutes, or until soy curls are crispy and golden brown. Remove from oven and set aside.

To prepare the sauce, combine water, liquid aminos, coconut palm sugar, lemon juice, sesame oil and tapioca starch in a bowl and set aside.

Heat oil or water in a large skillet on medium heat. Add onion and cook until soft, about 4 minutes. Stir in garlic, ginger and bell pepper and cook for 2 minutes. Add baked soy curls and cook, stirring 1 minute. Stir in sauce mixture and cook until thickened, about 2 minutes. Remove from heat and add green onions for garnish.

SPAGHETTI SQUASH PAD THAI

This is a healthier version of Pad Thai. It is also grain-free with the use of spaghetti squash. The reason I use spaghetti squash is because it turns into spaghetti-like strands when cooked. 1 cup of cooked spaghetti squash contains only 42 calories, therefore using it to replace grains in a meal greatly reduces the overall calorie content. This is my favorite dish for using up spaghetti squashes.

INGREDIENTS:

1 small spaghetti squash (1-2 pounds/454-908g)
1 tablespoon olive oil or ¼ cup water
4 sliced green onions (white and green parts)
4 cloves garlic, minced
1 inch ginger, grated
¼ cup (39g) lima beans
1 cup (89g) green cabbage, thinly sliced
1 small carrot, cut into matchsticks
¼ cup (110g) snow peas, cut into strips
1 cup (149g) red bell pepper, thinly sliced
¼ cup (22g) roasted peanuts
¼ cup (4g) chopped cilantro (optional)
Sauce
1 tablespoon sesame oil
2 tablespoons Bragg's liquid aminos or 1 tablespoon soy sauce
2 tablespoons natural peanut butter
1 tablespoon lemon juice
2 tablespoons maple syrup
Pinch Cayenne pepper (optional)

DIRECTIONS:

Preheat oven 400°F/200°C. Prick spaghetti squash, place on a baking sheet and roast for about 1 hour, or until tender. Combine sauce ingredients in a bowl and mix until creamy, then set aside. Heat olive oil or water in a large skillet on medium heat. Add spring onion, garlic and ginger. Cook, stirring constantly, for 2 minutes, or until fragrant. Add lima beans, cabbage, carrots, snow peas, and red bell pepper and cook for 5 minutes, constantly stirring.

Remove squash from the oven and allow to cool enough to be handled. Cut squash in half lengthwise and using a fork, scoop out the seeds and discard. Use the fork to scrape flesh to remove spaghetti strands. Add spaghetti squash and sauce to vegetables, stirring to evenly coat, and until squash is fully heated through. Remove from heat and garnish with peanuts and cilantro.

SPINACH ARTICHOKE LASAGNA

When I decided to transition into eating a plant-based diet, giving up cheese was my most difficult challenge. Honestly, it was the final hurdle for me. I do understand how difficult it is for others who are on this journey to a plant-based diet. I spent hours in the kitchen experimenting with alternatives and soon I enjoyed the plant-based versions better. I especially loved the way eating plant-based alternatives made me feel. This is a tasty and pleasing variation to the regular way of making vegan lasagnas. It is creamy and rich and especially great when you have company. You can top it with your favorite vegan cheese. Make sure to use gluten-free lasagna noodles or substitute with fresh zucchini noodles.

INGREDIENTS:

Cheese Sauce
1 cup (125g) raw cashew, soaked for 1 hour
1 cup (240ml) water
1 tablespoon tapioca starch
3 cloves garlic
¼ cup (39g) red bell pepper
2 tablespoons nutritional yeast flakes
2 tablespoons lemon juice
1 teaspoon dried basil
½ teaspoon parsley flakes
1½ teaspoons sea salt

Lasagna
1 tablespoon olive oil or ¼ cup water
1 onion, chopped finely
2 cloves garlic, minced
1 small red bell pepper, chopped
1 (14 ounce/ 400g) can artichoke hearts, drained and chopped
2 handfuls of spinach leaves
½ teaspoon sea salt
3 cups (732g) of your favorite pasta or marinara sauce
1 (10-ounce/220g) package gluten-free lasagna noodles (oven-ready)
1 cup (112g) shredded vegan 'cheese' (optional)

DIRECTIONS:

To make the cheese sauce, rinse and drain raw cashews, and place in a high speed blender with the remaining ingredients. Process until smooth. Set aside.

Preheat the oven at 400°F/200°C. Heat olive oil or water in a large skillet on medium heat. Add onions and cook, stirring until soft, for about 4 minutes. Stir in garlic and red bell pepper and cook for another minute. Add artichoke hearts and spinach and cook until spinach leaves are wilted. Season with salt to taste.

To assemble: Evenly spread one cup of tomato sauce on the bottom of a 9x13 casserole dish. Layer lasagna noodles on top, then add half of the cheese sauce, followed by half of the vegetables. Repeat layers with pasta sauce, noodles, the remaining cheese sauce, the remaining vegetables, and ending with tomato sauce. Sprinkle top with vegan cheese shreds, and bake covered with foil for about 45 minutes. Cool for 15 minutes before serving.

DIRECTIONS:

Preheat oven 400°F/200°C. Using a fork, pierce each potato and place on a baking sheet. Bake for 60 minutes or until baked through.

While potatoes are baking, heat oil or water in a medium saucepan on medium heat. Add onion and sauté until soft, for about 4 minutes. Add garlic and cook for 30 seconds. Stir in black beans, water and Italian seasonings cook stirring for 5 minutes. Prepare the cheese sauce.

Remove potatoes from oven, and let stand until cool enough to handle. Slice potato lengthwise. Using a fork, mash potato. Mound black beans, corn, tomatoes and avocados. Drizzle with bell pepper sauce and garnish with green onions.

Bell Pepper Sauce: Preheat oven 450°F/230°C. Line baking sheet with parchment paper. Place baking sheet on the pan and bake for 25 minutes or until brown. Allow to cool enough to handle. Slice bell pepper, remove stems and seeds, and place in blender.

Drain and rinse raw cashews, add to blender with water, onion, garlic and salt. Process until smooth. Pour into a small saucepan on medium low heat. Using a whisk, stir until sauce begins to bubble and thicken.

Sweet potatoes, loaded with seasoned black beans, corn, tomatoes, green onions, avocado and drizzled with a delicious red bell pepper sauce.

INGREDIENTS:

2 medium sweet potatoes, washed
1 tablespoon olive oil or ¼ cup water
½ cup (80g) onion, finely chopped
1 clove garlic, minced
1 ½ cup cooked or 1 (15-ounce/425g) can black beans, rinsed and drained
¼ cup (60ml) water
¼ teaspoon Italian seasoning
Sea salt
½ cup (62g) corn kernels
¼ cup (35g) cherry tomatoes, halved
1 avocado, chopped
1 chopped green onion (green part only)
1 cup (149g) bell pepper sauce (recipe follows)
Bell Pepper Sauce
1 red bell pepper, chopped
½ cup (62g) raw cashews, soaked for 2 hours
½ cup (120ml) water
1 tablespoon onion, chopped
1 clove garlic, chopped
½ teaspoon salt

THAI YELLOW VEGETABLE CURRY

When my husband took me to a vegan restaurant for my birthday, I was elated. As we sat down to choose, I asked the waitress what were the most popular dishes served in the restaurant. She said Thai Curry, Soba Noodles and Chili Fries. I happily chose the Thai Curry and was very pleased with my decision. The curry was very delicious, not too spicy, but not too sweet. It was a delicious blend of aromatics, coconut milk, lemongrass and basil. I told my husband that I definitely had to replicate this dish for my cookbook. Here is the result.

INGREDIENTS:

4 medium potatoes, chopped
2 medium carrots, chopped
1 cup (91g) broccoli florets
1 tablespoon chopped Thai basil
1 teaspoon coconut palm sugar
1 tablespoon Bragg's liquid aminos
2 cups (480g) water or vegetable stock
Salt to taste
Paste
1 tablespoon coconut oil
1 medium onion, chopped
2 cloves garlic
1 lemongrass stalk, chopped
½ inch ginger, chopped
1 ½ teaspoon ground coriander
1 teaspoon turmeric
1 teaspoon cumin
½ teaspoon lemon zest
¼ teaspoon Cayenne pepper

DIRECTIONS:

Place all the ingredients for the paste into a blender and process until smooth. Heat oil in large saucepan on medium high heat. Add paste and cook, stirring constantly for about 3 minutes. Add potatoes and carrots, stirring to coat. Stir in coconut milk, water, or vegetables stock, basil, sugar, and liquid aminos. Cook vegetables until tender, about 15 minutes. Stir in broccoli and cook for 2-3 or until tender. Season with salt to taste.

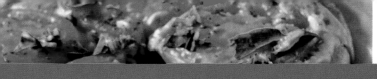

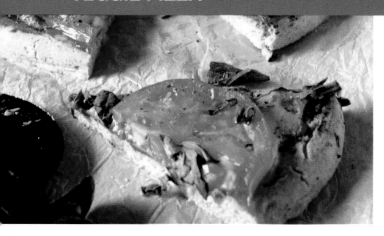

Here is a recipe I developed that allowed me to continue to enjoy my favorite dish, minus the abdominal discomforts of IBS after.

INGREDIENTS:

Crust
2/3 cup (90g) brown rice flour
½ cup (56g) almond meal
1/3 cup (60g) potato starch
2 tablespoons ground flax seed or white chia seeds
½ teaspoon baking powder
½ teaspoon sea salt
1/3 cup (75ml) non-dairy milk (almond, soy, coconut)
1/3 (75ml) cup water
1 teaspoon olive oil

Pizza Sauce
1 (8-ounce/217g) can of tomato sauce
1 (6-ounce/165g) can of tomato paste
½ teaspoon of basil
½ teaspoon oregano
¼ teaspoon thyme
¼ teaspoon fennel powder
2 cloves garlic, minced
¼ teaspoon coconut palm sugar
½ teaspoon sea salt

Cashew Cheese Sauce
½ cup (62g) raw cashews
½ cup (120ml) water
2 tablespoons nutritional yeast flakes
1 tablespoon lemon juice
½ red bell pepper
1 tablespoon onion, chopped
1 clove garlic
¾ teaspoon sea salt

DIRECTIONS:

Preheat oven 425°F/220°C. In a bowl, add brown rice flour, almond meal, potato starch, flax seed or chia seeds, baking powder, and sea salt. In a smaller bowl, combine milk, water and olive oil. Stir wet ingredients into dry ingredients, mixing well until fully combined. Roll out dough on a floured surface or between 2 parchment sheets to desired size. Carefully transfer dough to baking sheet or pizza stone and bake for 10 minutes.

Pizza Sauce: In a saucepan over medium heat, add tomato sauce, tomato paste, and the rest of the ingredients, stirring well. Bring to boil, and then reduce heat to simmer for about half an hour. Allow to cool.

Cashew Cheese Sauce: Drain cashews and add to a high speed blender with the remaining ingredients. Process until sauce is smooth and creamy. Transfer sauce to a small saucepan and cook on medium heat, stirring constantly with a whisk until sauce is thick.

Pizza Assembly: Vegetable toppings: Sliced tomatoes, blanched broccoli, and yellow bell pepper strips. On top of bake pizza dough, add pizza sauce, then top with cheese sauce and vegetable toppings. Return to oven and bake for 3-4 minutes, remove from oven then cool, slice and serve.

VEGETABLE BIRYANI

Biryani is a traditional Indian one pot main dish, consisting of cooked layers of rice and vegetables. This dish does take a while to prepare, but the resulting dish is well worth the time. It is best served at formal gatherings. I first enjoyed this dish when I visited Indian restaurants in England while I was studying there.

INGREDIENTS:

Rice
2 cups brown rice
3 cups water
1 bay leaf
1 ½ teaspoon sea salt
Vegetables
1 tablespoon coconut oil or ¼ (60ml) cup water
1 onion, sliced
2 cloves garlic, minced
1 teaspoon ginger, finely minced
¼ teaspoon ground cumin
1 teaspoon coriander
½ teaspoon turmeric, divided
½ teaspoon cardamom, grounded
1 medium tomato, pureed
2 cups (200g) cauliflower, cut into florets
1 medium carrot, diced
1 medium potato, diced
½ cup (55g) green peas

1 teaspoon sea salt
¼ cup (60ml) water
½ cup (62g) cashew mayonnaise
½ cup (8g) cilantro leaves
½ cup (8g) mint leaves
½ cup (62g) raw cashew as garnish
Pinch of Cayenne (optional)

DIRECTIONS:

Wash rice well, using a sieve under cold running water. Place rice, bay leaf, salt and water in a medium saucepan with tight-fitting lid on medium-high heat, and bring to boil. Lower heat to simmer for 50 minutes, or until rice is tender. Turn off heat and fluff with a fork. Set aside.

Heat oil or water in a large skillet on medium-high heat. Add onion slices and cook until soft for about 5 minutes. Add garlic and ginger, and cook for 1 minute, until fragrant. Add cumin, coriander, turmeric, and cardamom, then cook, stirring until toasted and fragrant, or about 1 minute. Chop tomato and place in a blender. Pulse to a puree. Add tomato puree to skillet and cook for 1 minute. Stir in cauliflower, carrots, potatoes, peas and salt. Add water and cook covered for 5 minutes. Preheat oven 350°F175°C. Remove lid and stir in cashew mayonnaise, mint leaves, and cilantro leaves, and cook for 2 minutes, then remove from heat. In a greased casserole dish, spread a layer of rice at the base, followed by a layer of vegetables over rice, then place a layer of rice on top. Cover and bake for 30 minutes. Garnish with cashews and serve.

INGREDIENTS:

1 cup (125g) raw cashews, soaked for 1 hour
½ cup (120ml) water
2 tablespoons tapioca starch
½ cup (120ml) almond milk
1 tablespoon lemon juice
2 teaspoons onion powder
½ teaspoon garlic powder
¾ teaspoon sea salt

DIRECTIONS:

Drain and rinse raw cashews. Blend cashew with water until smooth. Add tapioca starch, almond milk, lemon juice, onion powder, garlic powder, and salt, and process until smooth. Transfer liquid into a saucepan on medium heat. Stir constantly with wire whisk until sauce thickens. Cool completely and keep in refrigerator for up to 10 days.

I love to make vegetable curries and I have tried to curry almost all the vegetables and beans I get my hands on. Once you get a base recipe, you will be able to substitute with the vegetables of your choosing. Being from Jamaica, I love to add coconut milk to my curries for a creamy, slightly sweet flavor.

INGREDIENTS:

1 tablespoon coconut oil or ¼ cup (60ml) water
1 medium onion, chopped
3 cloves garlic, minced
1 inch ginger, finely minced
1 teaspoon ground cumin
1 teaspoon turmeric
2 teaspoons ground coriander
¼ teaspoon cardamom
1 ½ teaspoons salt or to taste
2 medium tomatoes, chopped
1 red bell pepper, chopped
1 medium potato, cut in quarters
1 medium carrot, chopped
1 ½ cups cooked or 1 15 ounce (425g) can chickpeas, drained
4 cups (120g) spinach leaves, stemmed, chopped
½ teaspoon Cayenne pepper (optional)
1 cup (240ml) coconut milk
½ cup (120ml) water

DIRECTIONS:

Heat oil or water in a large saucepan with tightly fitted cover over medium-high heat. Stir in onion and garlic and cook until onion is soft, or around 3 minutes. Add ginger, cumin, turmeric, coriander, cardamom and salt. Cook, while stirring, for 2 minutes. Add tomatoes, bell peppers, potatoes, carrots, chickpeas, spinach, and Cayenne, stirring to coat, for 2 minutes. Add coconut milk and water, then cover saucepan and bring to boil. Reduce heat to a simmer and cook for 20 minutes, or until vegetables are tender.

SALADS

Eating a salad before your main meal, helps to reduce your overall caloric intake. Due to its high fiber and water content, it makes you feel full faster so you tend to eat less of your main meal. Some of my hot salad recipes can be eating as a main meal.

ARTICHOKE GREEN BEAN AND POTATO SALAD   YIELD: 4 SERVINGS

This flavorful salad is delicious on its own or as a side dish.

INGREDIENTS:

4 red skin potatoes, cut in quarters
2 cups (220g) green beans, trimmed and cut in 2 inch lengths
1 (14-ounce/400g) can artichokes, drained and quartered
Dressing
2 tablespoons olive oil
2 tablespoons lemon juice
2 cloves garlic, minced
½ teaspoon parsley
½ teaspoon basil
½ teaspoon oregano
1 teaspoon sea salt

DIRECTIONS:

Place potatoes, covered with water, in a medium saucepan with tight fitting lid on high heat. Bring to boil, reduce to a simmer and cook until tender for about 20 minutes.

While potato is cooking, whisk together dressing ingredients and set aside. Remove potatoes to a bowl using a large slotted spoon, then return water in saucepan to a boil. Add green beans and blanch for about 2 minutes. Drain water, then rinse green beans with cold water. Drain green beans and add to potatoes. Add artichokes and toss in dressing, mix gently to coat.

BROCCOLI AVOCADO SALAD WITH SESAME TAHINI DRESSING

YIELD: 4 SERVINGS

A healthy and a nutritious salad, broccoli is packed with numerous nutritional benefits. To name a few, broccoli is a member of the cruciferous family and therefore has the same cancer fighting properties as cabbage, cauliflower and Brussels sprouts. Broccoli contains lots of fiber, which helps to lower cholesterol, aids in weight loss and helps to maintain regular bowel function. Broccoli also contains a good source of calcium and vitamin K, which helps to strengthen bone and prevents osteoporosis.

INGREDIENTS:

4 cups (364g) broccoli florets
1 avocado, peeled, pitted and cut into cubes
¼ cup (40g) red onion, chopped
Dressing
2 tablespoons tahini
2 tablespoons water
2 tablespoons lemon juice
2 tablespoons Bragg's liquid aminos or coconut aminos
1 teaspoon sesame oil
1 chopped green onion (white and green parts)
1 garlic clove, chopped

DIRECTIONS:

Bring a large saucepan of water to boil, add broccoli florets, and blanch for about 3 minutes, until light green and slightly tender to touch. Using a colander, drain and rinse with cold running water. Place broccoli florets in a bowl, and add avocado and red onion. Process dressing ingredients in a blender until smooth. You may need to add extra water. Pour dressing over broccoli salad and toss well. Serve immediately or refrigerate until ready.

COBB SALAD WITH SESAME DRESSING

For the sesame dressing
2 tablespoons lemon juice
2 tablespoons Bragg's liquid aminos or coconut aminos
1 tablespoon maple syrup
1 teaspoon sesame oil
1 clove garlic, minced
2 teaspoons ginger, grated
1 finely chopped green onion (white parts only)
Salt to taste

This is a healthier version of the famous American Cobb salad. The salad is traditionally made with lettuce, tomato, boiled egg, cheese, chicken breast, bacon and red wine vinaigrette. I loved the beautiful presentation of this salad, therefore I decided to make a vegan version. I added baked soy curls, corn, tomatoes, bell peppers, and avocados, topped with a sesame dressing on a bed of romaine lettuce. It was so delicious, I couldn't wait to make more.

INGREDIENTS:

For the salad
½ head romaine lettuce, washed and chopped
1 cup (125g) fresh corn kernels
2 cups (280g) grape tomatoes, cut in halves
1 orange bell pepper, cut into strips
1 avocado, pitted and chopped
1 cup (40g) baked soy curls

For the baked soy curls
1 cup (40g) Butler's soy curls
1 tablespoon nutritional yeast flakes
2 tablespoons Bragg's liquid aminos
1 teaspoon parsley
¼ teaspoon cumin
2 tablespoons tapioca starch

DIRECTIONS:

Prepare soy curls: Preheat oven 400°F/200°C. Prepare baking sheet with slightly greased parchment paper and set aside. Place Soy curls in a bowl and cover with warm water to rehydrate for about 10 minutes. Drain. Toss soy curls with yeast flakes, liquid aminos, parsley, cumin and tapioca starch. Place soy curls in single layer on baking sheet and bake for 20 minutes or until soy curls are slightly crispy and golden brown. Remove from oven and set aside.

Prepare dressing: Whisk dressing ingredients in a small bowl, set aside.

Assemble salad: Arrange lettuce on serving plate. Place corn kernels, tomatoes, bell pepper strips, avocados and soy curls in rows on top of lettuce. Pour sesame dressing on top and serve.

Marinated kale salad is another popular salad on my website. This version has way less ingredients but tastes just as delicious.

INGREDIENTS:

Marinade:
2 tablespoons olive oil
1 tablespoon maple syrup
1 tablespoon lemon juice
1/8 teaspoon sea salt or to taste
8 ounce (67g) bunch young kale, stems removed and cut into small pieces
½ cup (70g) cherry tomatoes, cut in halves
1 avocado, chopped
¼ cup (40g) red onion, diced

DIRECTIONS:

Place kale pieces in a bowl, and add olive oil, maple syrup, lemon juice, and sea salt. Massage kale. Add cherry tomatoes, avocados and red onion.

PINEAPPLE COLESLAW

YIELD: 4 SERVINGS

Take your summer picnic meals to another level with this pineapple coleslaw. It will add a tasty, mysterious bite to your veggie burger.

INGREDIENTS:

4 cups (356g) green cabbage, thinly sliced
2 small carrots, peel and shredded
¼ cup (22g) red cabbage, thinly sliced
1 cup (165g) pineapple, diced
1 tablespoon lemon juice
¾ cup (180g) cashew mayonnaise
¼ teaspoon sea salt

DIRECTIONS:

Mix cabbage, carrots, cabbage and pineapple in a large mixing bowl. Mix lemon juice, mayonnaise and salt in a separate bowl. Stir into coleslaw mix to fully combine.

INGREDIENTS:

1 cup (125g) raw cashews, soaked for 1 hour
½ cup (120ml) water
2 tablespoons tapioca starch
½ cup (120ml) almond milk
1 tablespoon lemon juice
2 teaspoons onion powder
½ teaspoon garlic powder
¾ teaspoon sea salt

DIRECTIONS:

Drain and rinse raw cashews. Blend cashews with water until smooth. Add tapioca starch, almond milk, lemon juice, onion powder, garlic powder, and salt, and process until smooth. Transfer liquid into a saucepan on medium heat. Stir constantly with wire whisk until sauce thickens. Cool completely and keep in refrigerator for up to 10 days.

This mouthwatering salsa is easy to make and is delicious served with tortilla chips.

INGREDIENTS:

2 cups (330g) fresh pineapple, diced
¼ cup (40g) onion, finely minced
½ jalapeno pepper, minced (optional)
2 tablespoons red bell pepper, chopped
2 tablespoons cilantro leaves, chopped
1/8 teaspoon cumin
1/8 teaspoon sea salt
½ lemon, juiced

DIRECTIONS:

Place ingredients in a bowl, then toss and refrigerate until ready to serve. Salsa will keep in refrigerator for about a week.

Chef's Tip: Prepare salsa at least 30 minutes before serving to allow flavors to marinate.

This is a delicious spin on the classic Middle Eastern dish, using quinoa instead of bulgur wheat. Quinoa is way more nutritious and gluten-free. I love to prepare this meal during hot summer months, using as many farm fresh vegetables and herbs as I can.

INGREDIENTS:

1 cup (184g) quinoa
2 cups (480ml) water
1 cup (140g) grape tomatoes, halved
1 cucumber, ends trimmed and cut into cubes
½ cup (80g) red onion, chopped
1 chopped spring onion (white and green parts)
¼ cup (4g) cilantro, chopped
¼ cup (4g) mint, chopped
1 avocado, peeled and diced
Dressing
2 tablespoons extra-virgin olive oil
2 tablespoons lemon juice
2 cloves garlic, minced
½ teaspoon cumin
½ teaspoon sea salt

DIRECTIONS:

Place quinoa in a fine sieve strainer and rinse under cold running water. Add quinoa to a small saucepan with tight fitting lid, then add water and bring to boil on medium heat. Reduce heat to a simmer and cook covered for about 20 minutes, or until quinoa is tender. Remove from heat, fluff with a fork, and transfer quinoa to a bowl. Allow to cool.

While quinoa is cooking, whisk dressing ingredients in a small bowl and set aside.

Add tomatoes, cucumbers, red onion, cilantro, mint, avocado and dressing. Toss gently to coat. Serve chilled.

Chef's Tip: Quinoa needs to be rinsed before cooking because it contains natural saponins, which act as an insect repellant. Place quinoa in a fine sieve and rinse with running water.

ROASTED BEET AND MINT SALAD

YIELD: 2 SERVINGS

Beets are by far one of my favorite vegetables. I love them roasted and tossed with a tangy dressing. I also love beet and apple juice. Yum! I can eat beets for breakfast, lunch or dinner.

INGREDIENTS:

4 medium beets
2 tablespoons olive oil, divided
¼ cup red onions, chopped
1 tablespoon maple syrup
1 tablespoon lemon juice
¼ teaspoon sea salt
2 tablespoons mint, finely chopped

DIRECTIONS:

Preheat oven 400°F/200°C. Prepare baking sheet with slightly greased parchment paper. Rinse dirt from beets. Trim tops and ends of beets and peel thin skin with a vegetable peeler. Cut beets in 1 inch chunks, and toss with 1 tablespoon olive oil. Bake for 50-60 minutes, or until tender. Remove from oven and toss with red onions, maple syrup, lemon juice, salt and mint. Serve warm.

ROASTED VEGETABLE QUINOA SALAD

Quinoa (pronounced 'keen-wa') is a natural whole grain gluten-free food that has been grown in South America for thousands of years. It is one of the few plants that is a complete protein. It is also loaded with fiber, minerals and vitamins. It is easy to prepare, and cooks much quicker than rice. It has a delicate, slightly nutty flavor.

INGREDIENTS:

½ cup (92g) quinoa, uncooked
1 cup (240ml) water
1 tablespoon olive oil
1 medium-sized sweet potato, peeled and cut in small cubes
1 pound (454g) Brussels sprouts, trimmed and cut in halves
½ teaspoon sea salt

For the dressing
1 chopped green onion (white and green parts)
2 tablespoons olive oil
2 tablespoons lemon juice
1 tablespoon ginger, grated
½ teaspoon sea salt or to taste
½ teaspoon sesame oil

DIRECTIONS:

Rinse quinoa with cold water using a fine mesh strainer. Add rinsed quinoa to saucepan with water, cover and bring to a boil. Reduce heat and simmer for 15 minutes, or until water is absorbed. Remove from heat and allow to stand for 5 minutes covered. Set aside.

Preheat oven 400°F/200°C. Place sweet potato and Brussels sprouts in a large bowl. Toss with olive oil and sea salt to combine. Transfer vegetables to baking sheet, spread in a single layer and roast for 20 minutes or until tender.

Place quinoa in serving bowl and add roasted vegetables. Combine well. Mix dressing ingredients in a small bowl and add to salad. Toss to combine.

Chef's Tip: Quinoa contains a bitter coating called saponin, which acts as a natural insect repellent for the plant. Easily remove this saponin by rinsing before cooking.

WARM ASPARAGUS SALAD

What better way to enjoy the flavor of asparagus than roasting them? Asparagus contains a powerful antioxidant called glutathione, which also acts as a detoxifier, protecting the cell from free radical damages and boosting the immune system. Asparagus contains inulin, which feeds the friendly bacteria in the large intestines. It is also a natural diuretic. Beware that in some people, eating asparagus can cause the urine to smell, but it is quite normal. Asparagus is a good source of dietary fiber, folate, and vitamins A, C, E and K.

INGREDIENTS:

1 pound (454g) asparagus, tough ends trimmed
1 tablespoon olive oil
¼ teaspoon sea salt
1 cup (30g) firmly packed spinach
1 avocado, diced
1 finely sliced green onion (white and green parts)
Lemon Dressing
1/4 cup (60ml) extra-virgin olive oil
2 tablespoons lemon juice
2 cloves garlic, minced
1 teaspoon maple syrup
1/4 teaspoon oregano
1/4 teaspoon sea salt

DIRECTIONS:

Preheat the oven to 400°F/200°C. Trim asparagus, cut in two pieces, place in a bowl, and toss with olive oil and sea salt. Transfer in single layer on baking sheet, and roast for 15-20 minutes, or until tender. Cut into 2 inch pieces. Place in a bowl and add the avocado, spinach, and green onion. Mix together lemon dressing ingredients and toss with salad.

SIDES

Delicious side dishes to accompany your main, or to be served alone or with a salad.

Golden crisp baked cauliflower fritters are a healthier version of the popular Indian spiced vegetable fritters. Vegetables are traditionally coated in a spicy batter, then deep fried until golden and crisp. Here I bake the cauliflower instead, so it is healthy and delicious.

INGREDIENTS:

2 cups (200g) cauliflower florets
½ cup (60g) chickpea flour
1 teaspoon turmeric powder
½ teaspoon cumin powder
½ teaspoon coriander powder
½ teaspoon sea salt
¼ cup (60ml) water

DIRECTIONS:

Preheat oven 450°F/230°C. Place lightly oiled parchment paper on a baking sheet. In a mixing bowl, combine chickpea flour, turmeric, cumin, coriander, and sea salt. Add water and stir well to form a smooth batter. Dip cauliflower floret into batter and transfer onto baking sheet. Repeat until all the florets have been coated. Bake for 15 minutes, then turn florets over and bake for another 15 minutes, or until florets are crisp and golden.

Two things are special about these fries. The first is they are baked in the oven instead of fried, and the second is they are tossed with garlic and cilantro.

INGREDIENTS:

6 Yukon gold potatoes, peeled and cut into thin strips
1 tablespoon olive oil
½ teaspoon sea salt
1 tablespoon nutritional yeast flakes
¼ cup (4g) cilantro, finely chopped
3 cloves garlic, minced

DIRECTIONS:

Preheat oven 425°F/220°C. Prepare baking sheet by lining with lightly greased parchment paper. In a large bowl, add potato strips with enough water to cover and soak for 30 minutes. This will remove excess starch from potatoes and result in crispier fries. Drain and rinse fries, then dry with kitchen/paper towel. Toss with olive oil, sea salt, and yeast flakes. Spread in a single layer on prepared baking sheet. Bake for about 35 minutes, until golden and crisp, flipping once after 15 minutes. Remove from the oven and lightly toss fries with cilantro and garlic.

This bread is moist, tender and delicious. It tastes better than any store bought brands. I used a combination of chia seeds and psyllium husk for bind and structure. You can substitute the chia seeds for flax seeds.

INGREDIENTS:

2 ¼ cups (540g) warm water (110-115 degrees F)
2 ¼ teaspoons active dry yeast (1 packet)
1 tablespoon coconut palm sugar
¼ cup (52g) ground chia seeds
2 tablespoons psyllium husks
¼ cup (60ml) olive oil
1 cup (140g) brown rice flour
1 cup (136g) sweet sorghum flour
½ cup (60g) buckwheat flour
½ cup (96g) potato starch
¼ cup (30g) tapioca starch
½ teaspoon sea salt

DIRECTIONS:

In a small bowl, add warm water, yeast, and sugar. Let sit for 5-10 minutes until mixture is foamy. Add chia seeds, psyllium husks, and oil. Set aside.
In a large bowl, combine brown rice flour, sweet sorghum flour, buckwheat flour, potato starch, tapioca starch and salt. Stir yeast mixture into dry ingredients, then knead until fully combined. Cover dough with damp cloth and place in a warm spot and let rise for 30 minutes. Remove from bowl and transfer to a greased loaf pan. Preheat oven to 350°F/175°C. Bake for 1 hour and 15 minutes. Remove pan from oven and place on a wire rack for 10 minutes. Gently remove bread from pan and cool completely before cutting. Store in an airtight container.

BROWN RICE PELAU

A flavorful version of a Caribbean rice dish, this is another dish that I love to prepare for a large crowd. It is usually gone in no time. The blend of flavors is out of this world. Traditionally, sugar is cooked in oil and allowed to caramelize to give the dish a dark brown color. I chose to omit this step and used molasses and coconut palm sugar instead.

INGREDIENTS:

1 tablespoon coconut oil or ¼ cup water
1 cup (160g) onion, finely chopped
3 cloves garlic, minced
1 cup (149g) red bell pepper, finely chopped
2 chopped green onions (white and green parts)
¼ cup (4g) cilantro or culantro, finely chopped
1 tablespoon fresh parsley, chopped
4 sprigs of thyme
1 small carrot, finely diced
1 cup fresh or 1 (15 ounce) can pigeon peas, rinsed and drained
2 tablespoons Bragg's liquid aminos
1 tablespoon unsulphured or pomegranate molasses
2 teaspoons coconut palm sugar
2 teaspoons sea salt
2 cups of long grain brown rice
1 (14-ounce/400g) can coconut milk

2 ½ (600ml) cups water
1 bay leaf
1 whole Scotch bonnet pepper

DIRECTIONS:

Heat a large saucepan with tightly fitted lid with oil or water on medium-high heat. Add onion and cook until soft, for about 4 minutes. Stir in garlic and cook for 30 seconds. Add bell pepper, green onions, cilantro, parsley, thyme, carrots, pigeon peas and cook for 2 minutes. Stir in liquid aminos, coconut palm sugar, sea salt, brown rice, coconut milk, water, bay leaf and pepper. Cover pot and bring to boil. Reduce to simmer and cook for 55-60 minutes or until rice grains are tender. You may need to add extra water, try ¼ cup at a time. Fluff with a fork.

Chef's Tip: If using dried pigeon peas, place in a bowl with about 3 cups of cold water to cover peas and soak them overnight. Discard water; bring 3 cups of fresh water to boil on medium high. Add peas and bring to boil. Reduce to simmer and cook until peas are tender, about 50 minutes. Drain and set aside.

Culantro and cilantro are both in the parsley family, but culantro has a more pungent scent and stronger flavor.

The addition of caramelized onions gives a sweet taste to this savory side; it will have your guests raving for more.

INGREDIENTS:

3 tablespoons olive oil or 1 cup vegetable broth, divided
1 large onion, chopped
8 medium potatoes
¾ cups (93g) raw cashews
1 cup (240ml) water
1 tablespoon lemon juice
1 teaspoon granulated onion
½ teaspoon granulated garlic
1 ½ teaspoon sea salt
¼ teaspoon dried dill weed
Chives to garnish

DIRECTIONS:

In a medium skillet, heat olive oil or ¼ cup vegetable broth on medium heat and sauté onions, stirring until golden brown, for about 30 minutes. Set aside. Peel potatoes, and cut in large chunks. Place in a large pot, cover with water and bring to boil. Reduce to a simmer for 20 minutes, or until tender but not mushy. Meanwhile, rinse raw cashews, and place in blender with water, lemon juice, granulated onion, granulated garlic and salt. Blend until very smooth and creamy. Drain potatoes and mash using a potato masher, stir in cashew sauce, caramelized onions, and dill. Decorate with chives and serve.

Chef's Tip: If using vegetable broth, add ¼ cup at a time, until onions are golden brown (you may need extra water).

This cornbread is a moist, flavorful blend of cornmeal and corn kernels sweetened with maple syrup and applesauce to ensure the bread is moist. If you prefer less sweetness, reduce the maple syrup to ¼ cup only.

INGREDIENTS:

2 tablespoons ground golden flaxseed or white chia seeds
¼ cup (60ml) water
1 ½ cup (198g) cornmeal
¼ cup (28g) almond meal
¼ cup (34g) sorghum flour
2 teaspoons baking powder
½ teaspoon sea salt
¾ cup (180ml) almond milk or other non-dairy milk
¼ cup (60ml) applesauce
¼ cup (60ml) coconut oil, melted
¼ cup plus 2 tablespoons (89ml) maple syrup
½ cup (62g) corn kernels

DIRECTIONS:

Preheat oven at 350°F/175°C. In a small bowl, mix flaxseed meal and water and set aside for 5 minutes. Ina a large bowl, combine, cornmeal, almond meal, sorghum flour, baking powder, and sea salt. In medium bowl, mix almond milk, applesauce, coconut oil and maple syrup. Pour the wet mixture, including flaxseed mixture, into the dry, and stir to combine, using a whisk. Fold in corn kernels and pour mixture into prepared 8x8 baking dish. Bake for about 55 minutes, or until toothpick inserted into the center comes out clean. Remove pan and let cool for 10 minutes.

Growing up in Jamaica, my mom always had a garden. She grew yucca/tapioca, which is also known as cassava in Jamaica. She would grow the tubers for use in making cassava pone, and for its starch. She used the starch for our clothes, especially our uniforms. Strangely though, I don't remember her cooking the tubers, except when we ate it in the form of Bammy. Years later, I had the pleasure of eating yucca with onions when a friend of mine from the Dominican Republic made it. She also prepared green bananas in a similar manner. That reignited my love for yucca.

INGREDIENTS:

1 pound yucca/cassava
2 tablespoons coconut oil
1 onion, sliced
3 cloves garlic, minced
1 lime, juiced
¾ teaspoon sea salt

DIRECTIONS:

Peel cassava, cut in chunks. Bring water to boil in saucepan on medium high heat. Cook until tender, for about 20 minutes. Drain water and set aside. Heat oil in a large skillet on medium-heat. Add onion and sauté, stirring until golden brown, about 10 minutes. Add garlic and cook for 30 seconds. Stir in lime juice and salt. Add yucca, stirring to coat and serve.

Chef's Tip: Yucca can be purchased in the produce section of most grocery stores, next to the potatoes and sweet yams. Also, you may find it in Asian or Indian grocery stores, fresh or frozen.

This fragrant and aromatic way of preparing potatoes is so easy to prepare and delicious. They are tender on the inside and crispy on the outside, and irresistibly good. Be sure to prepare extra.

INGREDIENTS:

6 small red potatoes
2 whole garlic bulbs, halved
1 lemon, thickly sliced
2 tablespoons olive oil
2 tablespoons lemon juice
1 teaspoon dried thyme
½ teaspoon dried rosemary
½ teaspoon sea salt
Fresh thyme for garnish

DIRECTIONS:

Preheat oven 425ºF/220ºC. Wash and dry potatoes, cut in halves and add to a bowl. Peel most of the outer layers of the garlic bulbs but leave the bulbs intact, then slice bulbs in halves and add with the potatoes along with lemon slices. Toss with olive oil, lemon juice, thyme, rosemary and salt. Spread on a baking sheet in a single layer. Bake for 45 minutes or until potatoes are tender, turning occasionally so that the lemons don't burn.

I love to make this dish using fresh bell pepper, squash, lima beans and corn. Whenever I serve this dish, it is always eaten up, without any leftovers. This dish is very popular in the southern states of the US, and was first made by Native Americans.

INGREDIENTS:

1 tablespoon olive oil or ¼ cup (60ml) water
1 medium onion, finely minced
2 cloves garlic, minced
1 cup (149g) red bell pepper, diced
1 zucchini squash, diced
2 cups (332g) fresh or frozen lima beans
2 cups (250g) fresh or frozen corn kernels
¼ cup (60ml) water
½ teaspoon dried thyme
1 teaspoon sea salt

DIRECTIONS:

Heat oil or water in a large saucepan on medium-high heat. Add onion and cook until soft, about 4 minutes. Stir in garlic and peppers, cook for 2 minutes. Add zucchini, lima beans, corn, and water. Cover saucepan and bring to simmer, until beans are tender, or about 3 minutes. Stir in thyme and salt to taste.

This dish is super easy to make and use with your favorite gluten-free pasta. I also added fresh spinach to the pesto sauce to boost the nutritional content of the dish. It is also a clever way to get children to eat their vegetables. You can substitute whatever nuts you have on hand to make the pesto, like walnuts, almonds, macadamia nuts, etc.

INGREDIENTS:

1 pound (454g) brown rice penne pasta
Pesto Sauce
¼ cup (31g) raw cashews, rinsed and pre-soaked
¼ cup (33g) pine nuts
1 cup (40g) basil
1 cup (30g) spinach
¼ cup (60ml) olive oil
1 tablespoon lemon juice
2 tablespoons nutritional yeast flakes
3 cloves garlic, chopped
½ teaspoon sea salt
¼ cup (60ml) vegetable broth
Pinch Cayenne pepper (optional)
¼ cup (54g) sliced black olives
¼ cup (35g) slices grape tomatoes

DIRECTIONS:

Bring a stockpot of salted water to boil (½ teaspoon salt). Add pasta and let it cook on high for about 12-15 minutes until pasta is al dente. Drain pasta and set aside until ready to use. In the meantime, drain raw cashews and add to food processor or high speed blender with basil, spinach, olive oil, lemon juice, yeast flakes, garlic, sea salt, and vegetable broth. Process until you have reached the desired consistency. Add pesto sauce to the noodles and stir well.

Jackfruit is grown in tropical regions of the world. The ripened fruit is more popular and it has a distinct flavor combination of mango, banana, pineapple and apple. The ripe fruit is used in a variety of desserts and even dried and sold as chips. The green (unripe) jackfruit is very versatile because of its meat-like texture and mild flavor. It is used as a popular meat substitute.

INGREDIENTS:

1 (20-ounce/565g) can of green jackfruit in brine
1 tablespoon olive oil or ¼ cup water
1 small onion, finely chopped
2 cloves garlic, minced
¼ teaspoon smoked paprika (optional)
¼ teaspoon Cayenne pepper
¼ teaspoon sea salt
½ cup (120ml) water
Barbecue Sauce
1 tablespoon olive oil or ¼ cup water
¼ cup onion, finely chopped
2 cloves garlic, minced
1 cup tomato sauce
2 tablespoons coconut palm sugar
1 tablespoon maple syrup
1 tablespoon molasses
2 tablespoons Bragg's liquid aminos
¼ teaspoon dried parsley
¼ teaspoon dried thyme
½ teaspoon sea salt or to taste

DIRECTION:

Drain and rinse jackfruit using a colander, and set aside. Heat oil or water on medium heat in a large skillet. Add onion and cook until soft, about 4 minutes. Stir in garlic and cook for 30 seconds. Stir in jackfruit and add smoked paprika, Cayenne pepper and salt, stirring to coat. Add water and barbecue sauce. Simmer, stirring until sauce thickens, for about 30 minutes. To serve, cut sandwich buns in half, top with barbecue jackfruit, followed with coleslaw on top.

Heat oil or water in saucepan on medium-high heat. Add onion and cook until soft, about 4 minutes. Stir in garlic and cook for 30 seconds. Add tomato sauce, coconut palm sugar, maple syrup, molasses, liquid aminos, parsley, thyme and salt. Simmer for 10 minutes until sauce thickens.

Chef's Tip: If you decide to use fresh green jackfruit in this recipe, please oil your hands, bowls, etc. when handling jackfruit. The unripe jackfruit has an exudate that is quite sticky. Green jackfruit can be purchased fresh, canned or frozen from Asian supermarkets.

These green beans can be ready to serve in minutes. Don't overcook them, only cook until tender. They should still have a bit of a crunch.

INGREDIENTS:

1 pound (454g) string beans, trimmed
1 tablespoon olive oil
4 cloves garlic, finely chopped
¼ cup (4g) cilantro (optional)
Salt to taste

DIRECTIONS:

Cook green beans in a large stockpot of boiling salted water, for about 5 minutes or until tender. Drain in a colander and put in an ice bath to stop the cooking process. Heat olive oil in a large saucepan over medium-low heat. Add garlic and cook for about 2 minutes, stirring frequently. Stir in green beans and cook until heated through, for about 5 minutes. Remove from heat, and stir in cilantro and salt to taste.

ROASTED RATATOUILLE

Ratatouille is a traditional French Provençal vegetable dish. Here, I use the roasting method in order to use less oil. This dish can be served as a side or main dish. This dish is reminiscent of my adventurous trips to Paris alone in my 20s. It is so strange now; I'm not sure if I would enjoy traveling alone now that I'm married and have children and I understand more about life.

INGREDIENTS:

1 medium eggplant, cut in ½ inch slices
2 zucchini, chopped
1 red bell pepper, chopped
1 yellow bell pepper, chopped
1 cup (140g) cherry tomatoes
1 red onion, chopped
10 cloves garlic, peeled
2 tablespoons olive oil
4 sprigs of fresh thyme, leaves removed
½ teaspoon dried oregano
½ teaspoon sea salt

DIRECTIONS:

Preheat oven 425°F/220°C. Line a large baking sheet with parchment paper and set aside. In a large bowl, combine vegetables and toss with olive oil, thyme, oregano and salt. Spread vegetables in a single layer on baking sheet and roast vegetables, turning a few times until they are tender and caramelized, for about 45 minutes.

This recipe for gluten-free sandwich roll yields a soft and moist bread. Gluten-free breads and rolls on the market are pretty expensive, so making your own is a great way to save on costs. I found that the addition of psyllium husk powder and flax seeds help to maintain the roll's structure. Psyllium husk powder may be purchased from the health food store or at Indian stores.

INGREDIENTS:

1½ cup (360ml) warm water
2 tablespoons coconut palm sugar
2 ½ teaspoons (7g) or 1 packet dry active rapid rise yeast
2 tablespoons olive oil
1 cup (140g) brown rice flour
½ cup (56g) almond flour
½ cup (60g) tapioca starch
¼ cup (34g) sorghum flour
¼ cup (48g) potato starch
¼ cup (40g) ground golden flax seeds
1 tablespoon (5g) psyllium husk powder
½ teaspoon sea salt
Sesame seeds (optional)

DIRECTIONS:

Heat water to 104°F. Stir in sugar and yeast, and then allow to sit for 3-5 minutes until mixture is foamy. Stir in oil and combine well with dry ingredients. The mixture will be soft. Cover bowl and allow to sit for 30 minutes to rise. Line baking sheet with parchment paper and grease well. Shape dough into balls with a greased hand. Place on baking sheet, cover loosely with plastic film. Allow to rise for 30 minutes. Bake in oven at 350°F/175°C for 20 minutes. Transfer rolls to wire rack. Best eaten within first 4 days.

I love to prepare this dish when I do catering events or serve a large crowd. It is flavorful and colorful. Filled with powerful antioxidants, it is definitely a winner recipe.

INGREDIENTS:

1 tablespoon coconut oil or ¼ cup water
1 medium onion, chopped
6 cloves garlic, chopped
1 tablespoon ginger, grated
½ cup (58g) red bell pepper, cut into thin slices
½ cup (58g) yellow bell pepper, cut into thin slices
¾ teaspoon turmeric
¼ teaspoon cumin powder
¼ teaspoon smoked paprika
¼ teaspoon allspice
¼ teaspoon cardamom
Pinch of Cayenne pepper
1 pound (454g) kale, trimmed, washed and chopped
1 cup (240ml) water
1 teaspoon sea salt

DIRECTIONS:

Heat coconut oil or water in a large skillet with a tight fitting lid on medium-high heat. Stir in onion and cook until soft, or about 5 minutes. Add garlic, ginger, bell peppers and cook for 2 minutes, stirring occasionally. Add turmeric, cumin, paprika, allspice, cardamom, and Cayenne pepper, and stir. Add kale and water, and cover and cook for about 10-20 minutes, or until kale is tender. Add salt to taste.

I would say this is one of the most popular side vegetable dishes served in Jamaica. It is usually served alongside spicy meat and fish dishes. The combination of cabbage and carrots brings out a sweet flavor that highlights the cabbage.

INGREDIENTS:

1 tablespoon coconut oil or ¼ cup (60ml) water
1 onion, thinly sliced
2 cloves garlic, minced
2 sprigs of thyme
½ head medium cabbage, washed and cut into thin slices
2 medium carrots, cut into thin strips
¼ cup (60ml) water
1 whole Scotch Bonnet pepper (optional)
¾ teaspoon salt or to taste

DIRECTIONS:

Wash cabbage and carrots and cut into thin strips and set aside. In a large saucepan, heat coconut oil or water, add onion and cook until softened for 4 minutes. Stir in garlic and thyme, and cook for a minute. Stir in cabbage, carrots and water. Cover the saucepan and cook until cabbage is tender, about 10 minutes. Add salt to taste.

One of nature's candies, sweet potatoes have been ranked number one in nutrition compared to other vegetables by the Center for Science in the Public Interest in Washington, D.C. Sweet potatoes are high in beta carotene, vitamin A, vitamin B6, vitamin C, fiber, thiamine, niacin, copper and potassium. They are also a good source of fiber, iron, calcium, vitamin E, and protein. Sweet potatoes, when eaten with the skin, contain more fiber than oatmeal. Sweet potatoes are especially beneficial for diabetics because they rank low on the glycemic index. They release glucose slowly.

INGREDIENTS:

2 large sweet potatoes
2 teaspoons organic tapioca starch
2 tablespoons extra virgin olive oil
½ teaspoon paprika
½ teaspoon onion powder
¼ teaspoon garlic powder
¼ teaspoon dried oregano
¼ teaspoon dried thyme
½ teaspoon sea salt or to taste
Pinch Cayenne pepper (optional)

DIRECTIONS:

Preheat oven 400°F/200°C. Line baking sheet with parchment paper and brush with oil. Wash and peel sweet potatoes, cut into thin strips about ¼ inch thick. Place potatoes in a large bowl and cover with water for about 1 hour to release the excess starch and sugars. Drain potatoes and use paper towel to dry. Lightly dust potatoes with tapioca starch. Drizzle olive oil and toss to coat potatoes, add seasonings and coat completely. Place on baking sheet in a single layer and bake for 30 minutes, turning after 15 minutes.

TERIYAKI BRUSSELS SPROUTS

YIELD: 4 SERVINGS

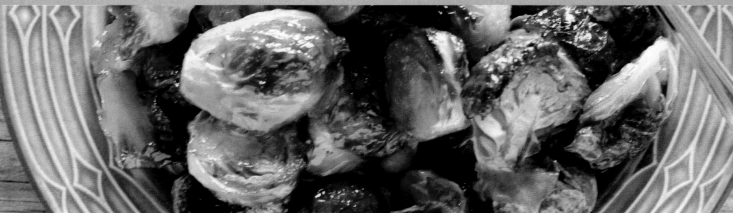

Brussels sprouts are among the most hated vegetables and have received a bad reputation for tasting horrible, bitter and sulfuric. Roasting them tends to reduce the bitterness and instead highlights the sweeter taste of the sprouts. By adding the right flavors to the sprouts, this tends to further enhance this vegetable and it will thus become a favorite of the pickiest eaters. Brussels sprouts are a good source of protein, iron, potassium, fiber, folate, antioxidants and vitamin C. They are low in calories and can be helpful as a part of a weight loss program. They are also helpful in preventing cancer, as well as other cruciferous vegetables, such as broccoli, cauliflower and cabbage.

INGREDIENTS:

1 pound (454g) Brussels sprouts, trimmed and cut in halves
2 tablespoons Bragg liquid aminos
1 tablespoon maple syrup
1 tablespoon coconut palm sugar
1 tablespoon olive oil
½ teaspoon sesame oil

DIRECTIONS:

Preheat oven 400°F/200°C. Place Brussels sprouts halves in a medium bowl. In a small bowl, combine sauce ingredients and stir. Pour the sauce over the sprouts and toss to combine. Spread on a prepared baking sheet and roast for 30 minutes, turning halfway.

SOUPS

Prepare a hearty and warming bowl of gluten-free vegan soup from my collection of delicious soups from around the world. From easy to prepare Mexican tortilla soup and red lentil and potato soup (Egyptian-Style).

BLACK BEAN CHILI

There is nothing like a colorful and satisfying bowl of chili, served with corn bread or rice. Extras can be refrigerated for up to 3 days.

INGREDIENTS:

1 tablespoon olive oil or ¼ cup (60ml) water
1 small onion, peeled and diced
3 cloves garlic, minced
½ medium red bell pepper, diced
1 medium tomato, chopped
1 cup (250ml) marinara sauce
¼ teaspoon smoked paprika
¼ teaspoon ground cumin
½ cup (12oml) water
3 cups (750ml) cooked or 2 (15-ounce/425g) cans black beans
½ teaspoon sea salt
¼ teaspoon Cayenne pepper (optional)

DIRECTIONS:

In a large saucepan, heat oil or water over medium-high heat. Add onion and sauté until soft, about 4 minutes. Add garlic and bell pepper and cook, stirring until vegetables begin to soften. Add tomato, marinara sauce, spices, water and beans and simmer for 20 minutes. Season with salt and Cayenne pepper to taste. To serve, ladle chili into bowls, garnish with vegan cheese and sliced green onions. Serve hot.

This soup is amazingly flavorful and is reminiscent of family, friends, and celebrations. I cook butternut soup similar to the way I cook pumpkin soup. Coconut milk adds just the right amount of sweet and creamy flavor to the soup. Feel free to substitute different spices in this soup. I tend to use allspice berries because I grew up using it. We actually had a tree growing at home. The berry is from the Jamaican bayberry tree and it has a sweet flavor, reminiscent of cinnamon, clove and nutmeg. This versatile spice is the key ingredient in Jamaican jerk sauce, spice cakes and German sausages.

INGREDIENTS:

1 tablespoon coconut oil or ¼ cup (60ml) water
1 small onion, diced
3 cloves garlic, minced
1 celery stalk, chopped
2 green onions, sliced (white and green parts)
1 tablespoon fresh parsley, minced
2 sprigs of fresh thyme or ¼ dried thyme leaves
1 small butternut squash, cut into chunks
1 pound (454g) potato, peeled and diced
1 carrot, diced
4 cups (960ml) vegetable stock or water
½ cup (120ml) coconut milk
1 whole Scotch bonnet pepper
Pinch of allspice (optional)
1 teaspoon sea salt

DIRECTIONS:

Heat coconut oil or water in a large pot, then add onion and sauté until soft, or about 4 minutes. Add garlic, celery, green onion, parsley, and thyme, and stir for 1 minute to release flavors. Add butternut squash, potato, carrots, vegetable stock, coconut milk, scotch bonnet pepper, and allspice. Cover and bring to boil. Reduce to a simmer and cook for 30 minutes, until vegetables are tender. Add salt, and remove scotch bonnet pepper and thyme sprigs. Puree half of soup, including vegetables, and return to pot.

Hearty and rich corn chowder, chock full of extra vegetables, such as zucchini, carrot, and potato. You may substitute your favorite non-dairy milk in this recipe.

INGREDIENTS:

1 tablespoon coconut oil or ¼ cup water
1 onion, chopped
3 cloves garlic, minced
2 finely chopped green onions (white and green parts)
1 medium zucchini squash, chopped
1 small carrot, chopped
1 medium potato, chopped
3 ears fresh corn or 1 ½ cups (188g) frozen
3 cups (750ml) water or vegetable broth
2/3 cup (80ml) coconut milk
1 bay leaf
1 teaspoon dried parsley
½ teaspoon dried thyme
1 teaspoon sea salt or to taste
¼ teaspoon Cayenne pepper (optional)

DIRECTIONS:

Heat oil or water in a large soup pot on medium-high heat. Add onions and cook until soft, or about 4 minutes. Add garlic and cook for 1 minute, then stir in green onions, zucchini, carrots, potatoes and corn kernels, cooking for another 3 minutes.

Add broth, coconut milk, and bay leaf. Cover pot and bring to a boil. Reduce heat to a simmer and cook for about 15-20 minutes, or until vegetables are tender. Stir in parsley, thyme, salt to taste, and Cayenne pepper.

Discard bay leaf and puree half of the corn chowder in a blender. Stir the pureed mixture back into the remaining soup. Ladle soup into individual bowls and serve.

CREAMY CAULIFLOWER POTATO SOUP

YIELD: 4 SERVINGS

This recipe is a very creamy and cheesy soup. If you love cheese, this is the ultimate cheesy-flavored soup. Even your non-vegan friends will enjoy this soup.

INGREDIENTS:

1 tablespoon olive oil or ¼ cup water
1 onion, chopped
2 cloves garlic, chopped
4 cups (400g) cauliflower florets
2 medium potatoes, cubed
2 teaspoons nutritional yeast flakes
2 cups (480ml) vegetable broth
Cashew cheese sauce (recipe follows)
Pinch Cayenne pepper, optional
Parsley for garnish

DIRECTIONS

Heat oil or water in a large saucepan on medium-high heat, add onion and cook for about 4 minutes or until onion is soft. Add garlic and cook for 1 minute, stirring. Stir in cauliflower, potatoes and yeast flakes, and blend to coat. Add vegetable broth, cover and bring to a boil. Reduce to a simmer for 15-20 minutes or until vegetables are tender. You may then process all the soup in a blender or remove half the soup to process. Return the processed half to the remaining half in the pot. Stir in cashew cheese and heat through. Serve with gluten-free croutons and chopped parsley.

CASHEW CHEESE SAUCE

INGREDIENTS:

1½ cups (188g) raw cashews, soaked for at least 4 hours
¾ cup (180ml) water
½ cup (74g) red bell pepper, chopped
2 tablespoons onion, chopped
1 clove garlic
2 tablespoons nutritional yeast flakes
1 teaspoon sea salt

DIRECTIONS:

In a blender, combine raw cashews with water and process until smooth. Add red bell pepper, onion, garlic, nutritional yeast flakes and sea salt. Continue processing until sauce is smooth.

MEXICAN TORTILLA SOUP

Hearty and comforting, this is my rendition of this classic Southwestern classic. You can make your own tortilla strips using corn tortillas or brown rice tortillas.

INGREDIENTS:

4 corn tortillas
1 tablespoon olive oil or ¼ cup water
1 onion, chopped
2 cloves garlic, minced
1 cup (140g) tomato, chopped
2 tablespoons tomato paste
½ teaspoon cumin powder
4 cups (960ml) vegetable broth
2 cups black beans, cooked or (1 14-ounce/425g) can, rinsed and drained
½ cup (62g) organic corn kernels
¼ cup (4g) cilantro, chopped
Pinch of Cayenne pepper (optional)
¼ teaspoon salt or to taste
Chopped avocado
Shredded cheese

DIRECTIONS:

Preheat oven 425°F/220°C. Slice tortillas into strips, and you may sprinkle with salt if desired. Lay in single layer on greased baking sheet and bake for 5-10 minutes or until golden brown. Remove from oven and allow to cool.

In a medium pot, heat oil or water on medium-high heat. Add onion and cook until softened, about 4 minutes. Add garlic and cook for 1 minute. Stir in tomatoes, tomato paste and cumin, cook for 1 minute. Add broth, black beans, corn kernels, and cilantro, stir to combine. Cover pot, bring to boil, then lower heat to simmer for 20 minutes. Taste and adjust seasonings. Serve soup ladled in bowls with avocado, cheese and tortilla strips.

This simple, delicious rendition of this Mexican soup is warming and comforting on a cold winter day.

INGREDIENTS:

1 tablespoon olive oil or ¼ cup (60ml) water
1 medium onion, chopped
2 cloves garlic, minced
1 stalk celery, chopped
¼ cup (39g) red bell pepper
¼ cup (39g) yellow bell pepper
¼ teaspoon cumin
½ teaspoon oregano
1 medium sweet potato, chopped
1½ cups cooked or (1-15 ounce/425g) can of pinto beans
3½ cups (840g) vegetable broth
½ cup (62g) fresh or frozen corn kernels

DIRECTIONS:

Heat oil in a large pot on medium heat. Add onion and sauté until soft, for about 4 minutes. Add garlic and cook for 1 minute, stir in celery, bell peppers, cumin, oregano, and sweet potato. Cook for 2 minutes. Add pinto beans and vegetable broth and bring to a boil. Reduce to a simmer and cook for 30 minutes or until desired thickness. Stir in corn kernels.

POTATO AND BUTTER BEAN SOUP

YIELD: 4 SERVINGS

The combination of potato, butter bean and coconut milk results in a rich, satisfying and creamy soup. This is the ultimate comfort soup in cold winter months. Butter beans are actually matured lima beans. They are white in color.

INGREDIENTS:

1 tablespoon olive oil or ¼ cup water
1 small onion, chopped
2 cloves garlic, minced
2 medium potatoes, peeled and chopped
2 medium carrots, chopped
2 celery stalks, chopped
2 chopped green onions (white and green parts)
2 sprigs thyme
2 bay leaves
Pinch of allspice
1 cup (240ml) coconut milk
1 cup (240ml) water
1 ½ cups cooked or 1 (15-ounce/425g) can butter beans, drained and rinsed
2 tablespoons Recipes Made Easy all purpose seasoning or vegan bouillon (optional)
Sea salt to taste
1 tablespoon potato starch plus 1 tablespoon water to thicken (optional)

DIRECTIONS:

Heat oil or water in a large pot over medium heat. Add onion and sauté until soft, for about 4 minutes. Add garlic and cook for 1 minute. Add potatoes, carrots, celery, spring onion, thyme, bay leaves, and allspice, stir to coat. Add coconut milk, water, and butter beans, bring to boil. Reduce to a simmer and cook for 20 minutes, or until potatoes and carrots are tender. Season with chicken-style seasoning and/or salt to taste. You may add potato starch mixture to thicken.

If you are using dried butter beans, sort 1 cup of dried beans and discard any debris or broken beans. Rinse beans and place in a bowl, add 3 cups of water to cover. Allow to soak overnight. The next day, rinse and drain beans until the water is clear. Place beans in pot along with fresh water, enough to cover beans at least 1 inch above beans. Bring to boil on medium heat. Watch the pot for a boil, then reduce to simmer. Cook for 40-60 minutes or until beans are tender, stirring occasionally.

Chicken style seasoning and vegan bouillon may be purchased at the local health food store or online.

SWEET POTATO AND RED LENTIL SOUP

This is a warm and hearty soup made of red lentils and sweet potato in flavorful spices. For this dish, I use the softer red lentils, because they don't require soaking before cooking and they cook in about half the time compared to other beans.

INGREDIENTS:

1 tablespoon coconut oil or ¼ cup (60ml) water
1 cup (160g) onion, chopped
2 cloves garlic, minced
2 teaspoons ginger, grated
½ teaspoon cumin
½ teaspoon curry powder
¼ teaspoon dried thyme
1 celery stalk, chopped
1 large sweet potato, chopped
1 medium carrot, chopped
1 cup (150g) dry red lentils, washed and drained
5 cups (1.2 liters) vegetable broth or water
½ teaspoon sea salt or to taste

DIRECTIONS:

Heat coconut oil or water in a large pot on medium-high heat. Add onion and sauté until soft, about 4 minutes. Add garlic and ginger, cook for 1 minute. Stir in cumin, curry powder, and thyme, cook for 1 minute. Add celery, sweet potato, carrot and lentils. Stir to coat for 2 minutes. Add vegetable stock or water, cover pot and bring to boil. Reduce to a simmer and cook for 40-50 minutes or until vegetables are tender and soup is thick. Add salt to taste.

Making your own vegetable broth is pretty simple. It is a wonderful way of using up older vegetables to make room for fresh ones. Vegetable broth adds flavor and nourishment to recipes and it can also be used as a substitute or to reduce the amount of oil needed in sautéing or frying in a recipe.

INGREDIENTS:

2 potatoes, including skin, washed and cut into large chunks
2 medium carrots, cut in large chunks
3 stalks of celery, cut in large chunks
1 onion, quartered
6 cloves of garlic, coarsely chopped
3 sprigs of thyme
1 tablespoon olive oil
4 sprigs of parsley
2 chopped green onions (white and green parts)
2 bay leaves
8 cups (1.5 liters) of water
1 teaspoon sea salt

DIRECTIONS:

Preheat oven 400°F/200°C. Place potatoes, carrots, celery, onion, garlic, and thyme in a large mixing bowl, then toss with olive oil. Place on a large baking sheet single layer and roast for 1 hour, turning every 20-25 minutes until golden brown.

Remove from oven and add roasted vegetables to a large pot, add water, parsley, green onions, bay leaves and salt. Bring to boil, then lower heat to simmer for about 1 hour.

DESSERTS

A presentation of desserts that are free of refined sugars, xanthan gum, guar-gum, hydrogenated-oils. Enjoy carrot cake with lemon cream frosting, ginger bread, coconut lime tart, Victoria sponge cake and strawberry thumbprint cookies . Now you can have your cake and eat it!

BANANA BREAD

My son Daevyd would make special requests for me to make this bread. It is super moist, delicious with banana flavors, and sweetened with maple syrup along with the very ripe bananas.

INGREDIENTS:

2 tablespoons ground flax seeds
¼ cup (60ml) water
1 cup (140g) brown rice flour
½ cup (56g) almond meal
¼ cup (34g)sweet sorghum flour
2 teaspoon baking powder
½ teaspoon sea salt
6 tablespoons (90ml) maple syrup
¼ cup (60ml) almond milk
¼ cup (60ml) coconut oil, melted
1 teaspoon vanilla
3 very ripe bananas, mashed

DIRECTIONS:

Preheat oven 350°F/175°C. Lightly oil a 9 x 5-inch loaf pan and set aside. In a small bowl, mix flax seed and water, and set aside for 5 minutes. In a large bowl, stir together brown rice flour, almond meal, sorghum flour, baking powder, and sea salt. In a smaller bowl, mix maple syrup, almond milk, coconut oil, and vanilla. Stir wet ingredients into dry and mix well. Stir in mashed bananas. Pour batter into loaf pan and bake for 1 hour or until toothpick comes out clean. Allow bread to cool in pan on wire rack before removing from the pan and slicing bread.

BANANA CREAM PIE

This is so much healthier and tastier than traditional banana cream pie, which contains refined sugar, egg yolks, butter, milk, etc.

INGREDIENTS:

Crust
1 cup (109g) pecan meal
¾ cup (45g) unsweetened coconut flakes
¾ cup (112g) dates
2 tablespoons golden flax seed meal
Pinch of sea salt

Filling
1 cup (125g) raw cashews, soaked for 4 hours
1 (14-ounce/400g) can coconut milk
¼ cup (60ml) maple syrup
2 bananas
1 tablespoon lemon juice
1 teaspoon vanilla
Pinch of sea salt
Banana slices for garnish
Coconut whipped cream for garnish

DIRECTIONS:

Place pecans and coconut flakes in a food processor and pulse until finely ground. Add dates, flax seed meal and salt, process until formed into a sticky ball. Press mixture into an 8 inch pie plate or spring form pan.

In a blender, process filling ingredients until smooth and creamy. Pour into prepared pie plate and freeze for about 6 hours. To serve, remove from freezer and allow to thaw for about 10 minutes. Garnish with banana slices and coconut whipped cream.

CARAMEL PUMPKIN PUDDING WITH COCONUT WHIPPED CREAM

This is an easy to make, delicious pumpkin pudding recipe that tastes like pumpkin pie, minus the crust. Coconut palm sugar gives the pudding a delicious caramel flavor.

INGREDIENTS:

1 (14-ounce/ 400g) can coconut milk
2 cups cooked pumpkin
2/3 cup (60g) coconut palm sugar
3 tablespoons tapioca starch or non-GMO cornstarch
1 teaspoon fresh ginger
1 teaspoon vanilla
¼ teaspoon sea salt

DIRECTIONS:

Place all ingredients into the blender and process until smooth. Pour into saucepan on medium-low heat. Stir constantly until pudding is thick, or for about 8 minutes. Transfer to individual serving cups and chill until set and firm, at least 1 1/2 hours. Top with coconut whipped cream.

CARROT CAKE WITH LEMON CREAM FROSTING

This delicious and moist carrot cake is sweetened with coconut palm sugar and frosted with creamy lemon frosting.

INGREDIENTS:

2 tablespoons ground flax seeds
¼ cup (60ml) almond milk
1 cup (140g) brown rice flour
1 cup (192g) coconut palm sugar
½ cup (56g) almond flour
¼ cup (30g) tapioca starch
¼ cup (48g) potato starch
1 tablespoon baking powder
1 teaspoon coriander
¼ teaspoon allspice
¾ teaspoon sea salt
¾ cup (180ml) almond milk
1/3 cup (75ml) coconut oil, melted
1 teaspoon vanilla
2 cups carrots, grated
Lemon Cream Cake Frosting
1 cup (125g) raw cashew nuts, soaked for at least 2 hours, rinsed and drained
2 tablespoons almond milk
1/3 cup (90ml) maple syrup
2 tablespoons coconut oil
2 teaspoons vanilla
1 teaspoon lemon juice
¼ teaspoon sea salt

DIRECTIONS:

Preheat oven 350°F/175°C. Grease an 8x8-inch baking pan and set aside. In a small bowl, mix flax seeds and ¼ cup almond milk, set aside for 5 minutes. In a large bowl, whisk brown rice flour, coconut palm sugar, almond flour, tapioca starch, potato starch, baking powder, coriander, allspice and sea salt.

In a separate bowl, mix remaining ¾ cup almond milk, coconut oil, and vanilla. Whisk wet ingredients into dry ingredients until fully incorporated. Fold in carrots and pour into prepared pan. Bake for 55-60 minutes or until toothpick inserted comes out clean. Cool cake completely before frosting.

For the frosting: place ingredients in a high speed blender and process until smooth and creamy. Place into the refrigerator for about 30 minutes to firm up.

Enjoy ice cream without the guilt. Coconut milk and cherries blend together in the creamy treat.

INGREDIENTS:

1 (14-ounce/400g) can of full fat coconut milk
1½ cup (138g) dark cherries, divided
¼ cup (48g) coconut palm sugar
2 teaspoons almond extract
Pinch of sea salt (optional)

DIRECTIONS:

Place ¾ cups of cherries, coconut milk, sugar, almond extract, and salt in your blender, process until smooth. Pour into a bowl and stir in the remaining cherries. Pour the mix into an ice cream machine and churn. Follow manufacturers' guidelines for the ice cream machine. Churn until the ice cream looks like soft serve ice cream. Transfer ice cream to a freezer-safe container lined with parchment paper and freeze for about 4 hours. Allow ice cream to stand for about 15 minutes before serving.

A perfect dessert to take you to the tropics with coconut and lime. If you don't have lime, substitute lemons.

INGREDIENTS:

Filling
1 cup (240ml) almond milk
1 cup (240ml) coconut milk
3 tablespoons tapioca starch
3 tablespoons maple syrup
2 tablespoons lime juice
1 teaspoon lime zest
Pinch of sea salt

Crust
1 cup (112g) almond meal
½ cup brown rice flour
¼ cup (28g) golden flax seeds, ground
1 tablespoon tapioca starch
¼ teaspoon sea salt
¼ cup (60ml) maple syrup
¼ cup (60ml) coconut oil, melted
1 teaspoon vanilla

DIRECTIONS:

For filling: Process all the ingredients in a blender. Transfer to a saucepan and cook on low heat, stirring constantly until thickened. Cool completely.

For the crust: Preheat oven 300°F/150°C. Lightly grease 4 mini tart pans or one 8 inch pie pan, set aside. In a medium bowl, combine almond meal, rice flour, flax seeds, tapioca starch, and sea salt. In a smaller bowl, mix maple syrup, coconut oil and vanilla. Add liquid to dry until fully combined. Using your fingers, press dough and shape dough into 4 mini tart pans or one 8 inch. Using a fork, make holes in the bottom of each tart. Bake for 12 minutes or until golden brown. Transfer to cooling rack, let cool for 5 minutes in tart pans. Remove and cool completely before filling.

To Assemble: Spoon cooled filling into each tart shell. Top with berries and serve.

134

This is another bread that is popular around the holidays. It's warm, spicy and full of flavors. You can substitute buckwheat flour for sorghum flour.

INGREDIENTS:

2 tablespoons ground flax seeds
¼ cup (60ml) water
½ cup (70g) brown rice flour
½ cup (70g) sorghum flour
¼ cup (30g) tapioca starch
¼ cup (48g) potato starch
¼ cup (28g) almond meal
¾ cup (134g) coconut palm sugar
1 tablespoon ground ginger
½ teaspoon ground allspice
2 teaspoons baking powder
½ teaspoon sea salt
1/3 cup (75ml) applesauce
¼ cup (60ml) coconut oil, melted
¼ cup (60ml) un-sulphured molasses
1 tablespoon fresh ginger, grated
¼ cup (60ml) water
Frosting
1 cup (125g) raw cashews, soaked at least 4 hours
¼ cup (60ml) almond milk or water
¼ cup (60ml) maple syrup
2 tablespoons coconut oil
1 teaspoon vanilla extract

¼ teaspoon sea salt

DIRECTIONS:

Preheat oven 350° F/175°C. Grease lightly a 9 x 5 loaf pan and set aside. In a small bowl, mix ground flax seed and water and set aside for 5 minutes. Whisk brown rice flour, sorghum flour, tapioca starch, potato starch, almond meal, coconut palm sugar, ground ginger, allspice, and baking powder in a large bowl and set aside. In a smaller bowl, mix applesauce, coconut oil, molasses, fresh ginger, water and flax seed mix. Add to flour mixture and mix well. Transfer to prepared pan and bake on the center oven rack for 55-60 minutes, until a toothpick inserted in the center comes out clean. Transfer pan to a wire rack and allow to cool completely before frosting.

Frosting: Place raw cashews, almond milk, maple syrup, coconut oil, vanilla and sea salt in a high speed blender and process until smooth.

JAMAICAN SWEET POTATO PUDDING

This is a popular pudding that's eaten all year long in Jamaica. It's traditionally made with wheat flour, but I substituted it with brown rice flour, tapioca starch, potato flour, and flax seed meal. The result was astounding and one could not really tell the difference from the traditional version.

INGREDIENTS:

2 pounds (0.90 kilo) sweet potatoes
½ cup (70g) brown rice flour
½ cup (60g) tapioca starch
½ cup (96g) potato flour
1/4 cup (28g) ground flax seeds
1 teaspoon baking powder
½ teaspoon sea salt
1 (14-ounce/400g) can coconut milk
2 tablespoons coconut oil
1 ¼ (240g) cup coconut palm sugar
1 teaspoon pure almond extract
2 teaspoons vanilla extract

DIRECTIONS:

Preheat oven 350°F/175°C. Grease a deep 9 inch cake pan or 9x5 bread pan and set aside. Finely grate potatoes using a box grater or a food processor. Transfer grated potatoes to a larger bowl. Stir in coconut milk, coconut oil, coconut palm sugar, sea salt, almond extract, vanilla extract, tapioca starch, potato starch, ground flax seeds and baking powder. Spoon batter in baking pan and bake for about 1½ hour or until knife inserted comes out clean.

Chef's Tip: For the authentic Jamaican taste it is better to use sweet potato variety found in West Indian and Asian grocers (also called batata). It has a red skin with white flesh and contains less water than the orange flesh variety found here in the USA.

136

OATMEAL RAISIN COOKIES

These oatmeal cookies are crunchy but chewy and sweetened with maple syrup and raisins for added sweetness.

INGREDIENTS:

2 tablespoons ground flax seeds
¼ cup (60ml) almond milk
2 cups (192g) gluten-free rolled oats
½ cup (70g) brown rice flour
¼ cup (48g) potato starch
¼ cup (30g) tapioca starch
1 teaspoon baking powder
½ teaspoon sea salt
½ cup (120ml) maple syrup
¼ cup plus 2 tablespoons (90ml) coconut oil melted
¼ cup (60ml) almond milk
1 teaspoon vanilla extract
½ cup raisins (50g) soaked in water for about 15 minutes

DIRECTIONS:

Preheat oven 350°F/175°C. Line a baking sheet with lightly greased parchment paper and set aside. In a small bowl, mix ground flax seeds and ¼ cup almond milk, set aside. In a large bowl, mix oats, brown rice flour, potato starch, tapioca starch, baking powder, and sea salt. In a medium bowl, mix maple syrup, coconut oil, the remaining ¼ cup almond milk, and vanilla. Stir in wet mixture along with flax seed mixture into dry ingredients to fully combine, and then fold in raisins. Spoon onto prepared baking sheet, using a tablespoon for smaller cookies, or an ice cream scoop for larger cookies. Bake for 15 minutes or until cookies are golden brown.

PEACH UPSIDE DOWN CAKE

YIELD: 1 CAKE

I love peaches in the summer and I can't seem to get enough of them. The sweet and juicy nectar is so good. I eat as much of them as I can fresh, and I try to incorporate them in as many recipes as possible. Instead of making a traditional pineapple cake, which was one of my childhood favorites, I used peaches instead. The outcome was a moist and tender cake.

INGREDIENTS:

Topping
2 tablespoons coconut oil, plus extra for greasing baking pan
¼ cup (48g) coconut palm sugar
2 tablespoons water
3 peaches, pitted and thinly sliced
To make the cake
2 tablespoons ground golden flax seeds
¼ cup (60ml) water
1 cup (140g) brown rice flour
2/3 cup (128g) potato starch
2 teaspoons baking powder
½ teaspoon sea salt
½ cup (120ml) almond milk
½ cup (150ml) maple syrup
¼ cup (60ml) coconut oil, melted
1 teaspoon vanilla extract
1 teaspoon lemon zest

DIRECTIONS:

Grease a baking pan with coconut oil and set aside. In a small saucepan, combine coconut oil, coconut palm sugar and 2 tablespoons water. Stir over medium heat until coconut sugar dissolves, then continue to cook, stirring until mixture thickens into a caramel. Pour caramel into prepared pan and allow to cool. Arrange peaches in a thin layer over caramel sauce and set aside while you prepare the cake batter.

Preheat oven 350°F/175°C. In a small mixing bowl, combine flax seeds and the remaining ¼ cup water and set aside for 3 minutes. In a large mixing bowl, combine brown rice flour, potato starch, baking powder, and sea salt. In a smaller bowl, combine almond milk, maple syrup, coconut oil, vanilla extract and lemon zest. Mix the liquid ingredients and the flax seed mixture into dry mixture with a whisk until fully combined. Pour cake batter over the peaches in the base of the baking pan.

Bake for 40 minutes, or until the cake springs back when touched or a toothpick when inserted comes out clean. Allow to cool for about 10 minutes. Run knife around the edges of the pan to release cake before turning until serving plate. Serve with ice cream or coconut whipped cream.

PEACH RASPBERRY CRISP

YIELD: 8 SERVINGS

Enjoy the bounties of summer with this peach and raspberry combo crisp. This dish tastes delicious on its own or served with ice cream. It can be served at breakfast, lunch or dinner.

INGREDIENTS:

Filling
4 cups (616g) peaches, peeled and sliced
1 cup (123g) raspberries, fresh or frozen
¼ cup (48g) coconut palm sugar
1 tablespoon lemon juice
1 teaspoon lemon zest
2 tablespoons tapioca starch
Topping
1 cup (96g) gluten-free rolled oats
1 cup (112g) almond meal
¼ cup (48g) coconut palm sugar
2 tablespoons maple syrup
2 tablespoons coconut oil
¼ teaspoon vanilla
¼ teaspoon sea salt

DIRECTIONS:

Preheat oven 350°F/175°C and prepare a 9-inch pie dish, set aside. In a large bowl, add peaches, raspberries, ¼ cup coconut sugar, lemon, lemon zest, and tapioca starch, and toss to combine. Pour mixture in pie dish and set aside. In a separate bowl, mix the oats, almond flour, ¼ cup coconut palm sugar, maple syrup, coconut oil, vanilla, and sea salt. Sprinkle topping over peach and raspberry filling. Bake for 25-30 minutes or until top is golden brown.

This cookie recipe allows the peanut butter to be the star because there are no competing spices added. Enjoy some 'peanut-ty' goodness. I also use maple syrup instead of sugar.

INGREDIENTS:

1 ½ cups (180g) oat flour
½ teaspoon baking powder
¼ teaspoon sea salt
1 cup (258g) peanut butter
½ cup (120ml) maple syrup
¼ cup (60ml) almond milk
1 teaspoon vanilla

DIRECTIONS:

Preheat oven 350°F/175°C. Line a baking sheet with lightly greased parchment paper. In a large mixing bowl, combine oat flour, baking powder and salt. In a medium bowl, stir together peanut butter, maple syrup, almond milk, and vanilla. Using oiled palms, shape into 1 inch balls and place onto baking sheet. Using a wet fork, flatten, making a crisscross pattern. Bake until edges are lightly browned, about 12 minutes.

This rustic tart gets to highlight the flavors of summer. I used Italian plums in this recipe.

INGREDIENTS:

Crust
1 tablespoon flax seed meal
2 tablespoons water
1cup (140g) brown rice flour
¼ cup (48g) potato starch
¼ cup (30g) tapioca starch
2 tablespoons coconut palm sugar
¼ teaspoon sea salt
½ cup (120ml) coconut oil
¼ cup (60ml) water

Filling
9 plums, deseeded and cut into slices
¼ cup (48g) coconut palm sugar
1 tablespoon tapioca starch
1 teaspoon lemon zest
Pinch of cardamom

DIRECTIONS:

Prepare Crust: In a small bowl, mix flax seeds and 2 tablespoons water and set aside for 3 minutes. In a large bowl, combine brown rice flour, potato starch, tapioca starch, coconut palm sugar, and sea salt. Add coconut oil, water and flax seed mixture, and stir by hand. Gently form into a dough ball (you may need additional water). Transfer dough onto parchment paper, lightly dust with flour, and roll out dough to ½ inch thick circle. Transfer to a baking sheet.

Prepare Filling: Preheat oven 375°F/190°C. Place plum slices in a bowl, add coconut palm sugar, tapioca starch, lemon zest and cardamom, toss to coat. Arrange plum slices in the middle of dough, leaving a two inch border. After filling dough, fold the edges up. Bake for 40 minutes. This is delicious served with coconut whipped cream or ice cream.

Even though these cookies are grain free, they are moist and delicious. Serve with your favorite all fruit jam.

INGREDIENTS:

2 cups (224g) ground almond
2 tablespoons tapioca starch
¼ cup (60ml) coconut oil
2 tablespoons maple syrup
1 teaspoon vanilla
½ teaspoon baking powder
Pinch sea salt
Filling
¾ cup (114g) fresh strawberries
1 tablespoon maple syrup
1 tablespoon chia seeds

DIRECTIONS:

Preheat oven 350°F/175°C. Place parchment paper on baking sheet. Mash strawberries with a fork. Add maple syrup and chia seeds, and mix. Allow to soak for 15-20 minutes while you prepare the cookies. In a medium bowl, mix almond, tapioca starch, baking powder, and sea salt. In a small bowl, mix coconut oil, maple syrup and vanilla. Stir into dry ingredients until well combined. Roll into balls and place on baking sheet about 2 inches apart. Using thumb, press in the middle to make an indentation. Using a teaspoon, drop filling into the middle of each cookie. Bake for 15 minutes or until golden brown.

VICTORIA SPONGE CAKE WITH COCONUT WHIPPED CREAM

This simple gluten-free cake is my go to recipe for a light cake. This recipe can also be used to make cupcakes. This cake contains maple syrup as a sweetener. Don't be deterred to make this cake.

INGREDIENTS:

2 tablespoons ground golden flax seeds
¼ cup (60ml) almond milk
1 cup (140g) brown rice flour
½ cup (96g) potato starch
¼ cup (28g) almond flour
¼ cup (30g) tapioca starch
2 teaspoons baking powder
½ teaspoons sea salt
¾ cup (180ml) maple syrup
½ cup (120ml) almond milk
¼ cup (60ml) coconut oil, melted
2 teaspoons vanilla
1 cup strawberry all fruit preserve or your favorite jam
Coconut whipped cream (recipe follows)

DIRECTIONS:

Preheat oven to 350°F/175°C. Lightly grease parchment lined baking pan and set aside. In a small bowl, combine flax seeds and almond milk and set aside for 5 minutes. In a large bowl, combine brown rice flour, potato starch, almond flour, tapioca starch, baking powder, and sea salt. In a medium bowl, mix maple syrup, almond milk, coconut oil and vanilla. Stir wet ingredients, along with flax seed mixture, into dry ingredients, and stir well to combine. Pour into prepared pan/pans.

Bake for about 16 minutes for cupcakes or 25 minutes for cakes. Cake is done when a tooth-pick inserted in the center comes out clean. Cool completely, then spread a layer of strawberry pre-serves over the top, topped with coconut whipped cream.

INGREDIENTS:

1 (14-ounce/400g) can full fat coconut milk
2 teaspoons maple syrup
¼ teaspoons vanilla extract

DIRECTIONS:

Refrigerate the can of milk overnight. Remove can and turn can upside down (this keeps the liquid on top). Pour off the liquid in a separate bowl and reserve liquid to be added to soups, stews or smoothies. Scoop out the remaining thick coconut cream in a separate bowl. Add maple syrup and vanilla and whip using a hand held mixer, or whisk until light and fluffy.

DIPS AND SAUCES

I prefer to make my own dips and sauces, they are fresh and you know all the ingredients that are in them unlike store bought brand. You can be creative and make different variations of your own.

This creamy and delicious artichoke dish is one of my favorite to serve for supper.

INGREDIENTS:

1 onion, chopped
4 cloves garlic, minced
1 (15 ounce/425g) can artichoke hearts, drained, rinsed and finely chopped
2 cups (60g) spinach, chopped
Sauce
½ cup (62g) raw cashews
½ cup (120ml) almond milk
1 tablespoon tapioca starch
1 tablespoon nutritional yeast flakes
1 tablespoon lemon juice
½ teaspoon onion powder
¼ teaspoon garlic powder
1 teaspoon sea salt

DIRECTIONS:

Preheat oven to 350°F/175°C. Place onion, garlic, artichoke hearts and spinach in a food processor or high speed blender and pulse until fully chopped. Transfer to a bowl. Blend the remaining ingredients until smooth. Stir into artichoke spinach mixture until fully incorporated. Spoon into lightly greased baking dish and bake for 20 minutes. Serve with tortilla chips or crudités.

BARBECUE SAUCE

INGREDIENTS:

2 teaspoons olive oil or 2 tablespoons water
2 tablespoons onion, minced
2 cloves garlic, minced
1 ½ cups tomato sauce
2 tablespoons maple syrup
1 teaspoon molasses
½ teaspoon cumin
½ teaspoon parsley
¼ teaspoon Cayenne pepper
½ teaspoon sea salt

DIRECTIONS:

Heat oil or water in a medium saucepan on medium-high heat, then add onion and cook until soft, for about 4 minutes. Add garlic and cook for 1 minute while stirring. Add tomato sauce, maple syrup, molasses, cumin, parsley, Cayenne pepper and salt. Bring to boil, lower heat to simmer for 10 minutes or until sauce is thickened.

This is a delicious and flavorful gravy. It can be served with mashed potatoes, tofu, biscuits or a part of your holiday meal.

INGREDIENTS:

3 tablespoons olive oil
¼ cup onion, finely minced
2 cloves garlic, minced
¼ cup (35g) brown rice flour
1 tablespoon nutritional yeast flakes
2 cups (480ml) water
3 tablespoons Bragg's liquid aminos
¼ teaspoon dried thyme
¼ teaspoon dried rosemary
Pinch rubbed sage

DIRECTIONS:

Heat oil in a medium saucepan on medium heat. Add onion and cook until onion is soft, about 4 minutes. Stir in garlic and cook for 30 seconds. Add brown rice flour and nutritional yeast flakes, stirring constantly for 4 minutes until paste is golden and fragrant. Add water, liquid aminos, thyme, rosemary, sage and whisk constantly until smooth. Bring gravy to a boil, then reduce heat to a simmer and cook for 4 minutes until desired texture is reached.

CARAMELIZED ONION AND ROASTED GARLIC HUMMUS

The sweet taste of caramelized onions and roasted garlic combines well in this hummus. Transform your plain hummus into a gourmet treat.

INGREDIENTS:

1 head of garlic
1 teaspoon olive oil
1 tablespoon coconut oil or ¼ vegetable broth
1 medium onion, diced
1 ½ cups cooked chickpeas or 1 (15 ounce/425g) can drained and rinsed
2 tablespoons lemon juice
2 tablespoons tahini paste
1 clove garlic
1 teaspoon sea salt or to taste
2-4 tablespoons water (optional)

DIRECTIONS:

Preheat oven 400°F/200°C. Peel outer garlic skin, leaving the bulb intact. Cut around ¼ inch off the top of garlic. Rub olive oil over garlic. Place cut side down on baking tray and roast in oven for 30 minutes or until tender. Remove from oven and allow garlic to cool. Squeeze out garlic.

While garlic is roasting, heat coconut oil in a medium saucepan on medium high heat, then add onion, and cook while stirring until brown. Reduce heat and continue stirring for about 20 minutes. Transfer to a plate and allow to cool.

In a food processor, combine garlic, onion, chickpeas, lemon juice, tahini, garlic, sea salt and water. Process until smooth. You may need to add extra water for desired smoothness. Garnish with caramelized onions.

CASHEW MAYONNAISE

INGREDIENTS:

1 cup (125g) raw cashews, soaked for 1 hour
½ cup (120ml) water
2 tablespoons tapioca starch
½ cup (120ml) almond milk
1 tablespoon lemon juice
2 teaspoons onion powder
½ teaspoon garlic powder
¾ teaspoon sea salt

DIRECTIONS:

Drain and rinse raw cashews. Blend cashew with water until smooth. Add tapioca starch, almond milk, lemon juice, onion powder, garlic powder, and salt, and process until smooth. Transfer liquid into a saucepan on medium heat. Stir constantly with wire whisk until sauce thickens. Cool completely and keep in refrigerator for up to 10 days.

CASHEW CHEESE SAUCE

INGREDIENTS:

1½ cup (188g) raw cashews, soaked for at least 4 hours
¾ cup (180ml) water
½ cup (58) red bell pepper, chopped
2 tablespoons onion
1 clove garlic
2 tablespoons nutritional yeast flakes
1 teaspoon sea salt

DIRECTIONS:

In a blender, combine raw cashews with water and process until smooth. Add red bell pepper, onion, garlic, nutritional yeast flakes and sea salt. Continue processing until sauce is smooth.

GUACAMOLE

INGREDIENTS:

4 ripe avocados
2 chopped green onions (white and green parts)
1 clove garlic, minced
1 lime, zest and juice
½ cup (8g) cilantro, chopped
1 tomato, chopped
½ teaspoon sea salt or to taste
Pinch Cayenne pepper (optional)

DIRECTIONS:

Cut avocados in halves and remove pits. Scoop out avocado into a bowl and mash with a fork or potato masher. Add onions, garlic, lime, and cilantro, and stir to incorporate. Fold in tomatoes, then season with salt and Cayenne pepper to taste.

LEMON SALAD DRESSING

This easy and fresh salad dressing taste better than any bottled dressing in the store. You may substitute the maple syrup with your favorite sweetener. This is my quick and easy go to recipe.

INGREDIENTS:

¼ cup (60ml) extra-virgin olive oil
2 tablespoons lemon juice
2 cloves garlic, minced
1 teaspoon maple syrup
¼ teaspoon oregano
¼ teaspoon sea salt

DIRECTIONS:

Mix together lemon dressing ingredients in a container with tight-fitting lid (such as a mason jar). Shake vigorously to blend flavors and toss with salad. Store in refrigerator for up to 3 days.

Making your own marinara sauce is worth the effort. I love to use my fresh, vine-ripened tomatoes for making sauce and making larger batches for canning.

INGREDIENTS:

3 pounds (1.3 kilo) fresh roma tomatoes
1 tablespoon olive oil or ¼ cup water
1 large onion, minced
4 cloves garlic, minced
1 carrot, finely grated
¼ cup fresh basil
1 sprig thyme
1 teaspoon dried rosemary
1 teaspoon dried oregano
1 tablespoon maple syrup
¾ teaspoon sea salt

DIRECTIONS:

Bring pot of water to boil, fill a bowl with ice water. Make an x with a knife at the bottom of the tomatoes. Gently lower tomatoes 3 at a time with a large slotted spoon into boiling water for approximately 15 seconds. Transfer tomatoes to cold water using slotted spoon, leave in cold water for 15 seconds then place them into another bowl. Repeat until all the tomatoes have been blanched and immersed into ice water. Remove the tomato skins, seeds and chop.

Heat olive oil or water in a large pot on medium heat. Add onion and cook until soft, about 4 minutes. Stir in garlic and cook for 30 seconds. Add carrots and cook for 1 minutes stirring. Add herbs and tomatoes and simmer for 1 hour. Stir in maple syrup and season with salt.

Chef's Tip: Use really ripe tomatoes for a better flavor and a bright red sauce. Sauce will last about a week in the refrigerator.

154

RESOURCES

For more information, recipes, natural remedies and skin care tips:
Healthier Steps
http://www.healthiersteps.com

Arrowhead Mills
Gluten-free flours, grains, seeds
The Hain Celestial Group, Inc.
4600 Sleepytime Dr. Boulder, CO, 80301
http://www.arrowheadmills.com/
1-800-434-4246

Bob's Red Mill
Gluten-free flours, nutritional yeast flakes, mixes,
grains, seeds
5000 SE International Way Milwaukie, OR, 97222
http://www.bobsredmill.com/Gluten-Free
1-800-349-2173

Bragg
Liquid aminos
http://www.bragg.com/

Coconut Secret
Coconut aminos, coconut nectar, coconut crystals,
coconut flour
https://www.coconutsecret.com
1-888 - 369-3393

Daiya
Vegan cheese, cream cheese, pizza
http://us.daiyafoods.com/

Healing Vineyard
Recipes Made Easy All Purpose Seasoning
https://www.healingvineyard.com

Trader Joes
Organic produce, grains, nuts, seeds, oils
http://www.traderjoes.com/

Whole Foods Market
(Organic produce, gluten-free flours, grains,
seeds, oils)
http://www.wholefoodsmarket.com/values-matter

Tropical Traditions
Coconut oil, red palm oil
http://www.tropicaltraditions.com/

ACKNOWLEDGEMENTS

Special thanks to all those who supported me with this endeavor. Thanks to Leilani Hortaleza, who has helped me at the conception of this book. Shaun McKeown, who wrote the first draft of the introduction. Special thanks to my brother Kemory Grubb for the layout and formatting, and cover design. Thanks also to my editor and copyeditor, Special thanks to my taste testers, hubby Devon and children Devannah and Daevyd.

ABOUT THE AUTHOR

Michelle Blackwood, a gluten free and vegan food blogger at www.healthiersteps. com. She is also a registered nurse, is dedicated to encouraging and helping people live a healthier lifestyle. Michelle's near death experience after the delivery of her son, and a bout with IBS, awakened a passion within her to share about health and how to use simple natural foods and remedies. She does cooking classes, health coaching, talks on health, and catering. This passion has also led her to create a line of natural skincare products, free of harsh sulfates, alcohol, or parabens. She grows some of her own foods and shops at local farmers markets. She lives with her husband and 2 beautiful children on 88 acres of land in the beautiful countryside outside Columbus, Ohio.

Index

vanilla extract 12, 13
VEGETABLE BIRYANI 83
vegetable broth 7, 62, 72, 73, 103, 108,
       120, 121, 123, 124, 126, 127, 149
VEGETABLE BROTH 127
VEGETABLE CURRY 85
vegetable stock 53
VEGGIE PIZZA 82
VICTORIA SPONGE CAKE WITH
       COCONUT WHIPPED
       CREAM 143

W

WAFFLE WITH BLACKBERRY
       SAUCE 31
walnut 25
walnuts 22, 27
WARM ASPARAGUS SALAD 97
WATERMELON GINGER BEER 41
white chia seeds. *See* chia seeds

Y

yeast flakes 10, 19, 20, 25, 28, 54, 56,
       57, 58, 59, 60, 62, 67, 72, 73, 75,
       77, 79, 82, 89, 100, 108, 121, 122,
       146, 148, 151, 155
yucca. *See* cassava
Yukon gold potatoes 100

Z

zucchini squash 107

Made in the USA
Middletown, DE
10 November 2019